"I believe that God is moving in s~~~~~~~~~~~~~~right now that are positioning His church for the greatest harvest of souls our world has ever seen. I am convinced that we will only realize the full potential of this season as we take our place in prayer as "Watchmen" over our communities.

I have seen firsthand the impact of unrelenting prayer leadership in our church and community. Dr. Susan Rowe and her husband Dr. Fred Rowe said yes to God's clear call to lead a prayer movement many years ago in our city. As a result unexplainable doors have opened, unimaginable resources have been given and otherwise impossible victories have been won.

As you read Remnant Rising you will hear the heart of seasoned prayer leaders who have a word from God for this vitally important moment in the life of the Christian church."

Wendell Vinson
Canyon Hills Assembly of God
Senior Pastor

"The raising of a remnant responding to the call of "Watchmen" in our time enlightens the open minded to a "new thing" God is doing. The book tells the compelling story of the journey of a watchman. The author provides a clear biblical perspective of what it means to be a watchman then expands the calling forth of a community committed to prayer illustrating from what took place in Herrnhut, Germany, which means "the Lord's watch" launching 24/7 prayer which lasted 150 years and the launch of estimated 3,000 missionaries along with the core principle "There can be no Christianity without community."

Luis Bush,
International Facilitator, Transform World Connections

"A powerful and clarion call for sustained intercession with focus on the 4th watch (3am-6am). The 4th watch has been recognized by many prophetic seers as a period of heightened spiritual activities. Throughout church history, the Holy Spirit has raised up pre-dawn prayer watches to catalyze movements of revival. The timing of the release of this book is crucial and its message is pertinent to this hour. I recommend this book to everyone who desires to grow in prayer and to see ubiquitous culture of prayer in the Ekklesia (church)"

Daniel Lim

CEO, International House of Prayer, Kansas City

"I will never forget the overwhelming sense of grace and gratitude that I felt standing in Newlands Stadium in Cape Town South, on the 21st March 2001, when 45,000 people convened for a day of prayer, repentance and reconciliation. This event was the birth date of the Global Day of Prayer that within 10 years would include every country on the face of the earth.

What started as an act of obedience ended up being a clarion call for believers from every continent to join the movement and to take their place as watchmen on the wall of the nations.

As the movement spread, so did my appreciation for what God was doing around the world. In this book '*Remnant Rising*' Susan Rowe and Greg Simas have clearly studied the history of prayer revivals and imparted a vision for the future. They have filled my heart with a sense of expectation as we watch and wait for the Body of Christ to *Ignite the Night and Awaken the Dawn.*

There is no doubt in my mind that we are living in the end times and therefore it is the responsibility of every believer to transform their world and to take their place as Watchmen, watching and waiting for His return.

Susan and Greg have an inspiring story and every believer who has a heart to see revival will enjoy this wonderful book."

Graham Power

Founder Global Day of Prayer & Unashamedly Ethical

Cape Town, South Africa

Remnant Rising

Remnant Rising

A Watchman Call to the Nations

Susan Rowe
With
Pastor Gregory Simas

Published in the United States of America

ISBN-13: 9781545303535
ISBN-10: 1545303533

DEDICATION

To my husband, Frederic, whose steadfast faith through the years is the back-bone of our ministry. Without his support, the experiences and revelation in this book could not have been written. He is a "man of peace," that has held a relentless pursuit of God throughout this journey with integrity and steadfast faithfulness. Similarly, I dedicate this book to our three sons who are diligently pursuing their life course with the Lord. May our watchfulness ever propel them into the fullness of God's purposes and plans for them. I hold a deep love and respect for each one of them.

Also, my deepest regard, respect, and thankfulness to a diligent prayer team whose life-sustaining prayers are interwoven throughout this book.

Finally, I want to dedicate the words of the book to those who will read it. May a Habakkuk 2: 2 commission fall upon you to "Run with the vision," to build and establish it.

ACKNOWLEDGEMENTS

Contributions by Pastor Greg Simas:

Greg Simas and his wife Wendi are the Founders and Senior Leaders of Convergence House of Prayer in Fremont, California. Their vision and mission is to see the glory and presence of the Lord fill the earth resulting in a global awakening that transforms cities and nations. Greg and Wendi have three children and four grandchildren.

Cover photo:
The cover photo was taken on an early Sunday morning prayer drive, November 29, 2014. The flame appeared the morning after "Watchmen" from across the state met in our city. It appeared at dawn, traveled slowly eastward and stayed in the sky well over 30 minutes. We honestly don't know how long it stayed, but photos taken 20-30 minutes later showed it had traveled distinctly East with no evidence of its source. The photo is untouched.

FORWARD

Have you ever wondered what the end-time harvest looks like? There have been many words, sermons, books written on the subject. Even now the question is rising in conversations as God draws our attention to the issue. What did Jesus see when He looked over the plains of Samaria. Here, in a desolate rather forbidden place, He said to His disciples, "Do you not say, 'There are still four months and then comes the harvest?' Behold, I say to you, lift up your eyes and look at the fields, for they are already white for harvest!" John 4:35. He saw a city ready for the harvest. He used the most unusual of places, with a most unexpected person, a prostitute, to reap a harvest of souls.

Today, as we look over the horizon of our lives, cities, nations, what do we see? Do we see the harvest? If so, are we ready? Is the body of Christ, His church, prepared to receive the lost and forsaken? Revelation 14:14-15 prophecies of such a time:

> "Then I looked, and behold, a white cloud, and on the cloud sat One like the Son of Man, having on His head a golden crown, and in His hand a sharp sickle. And another angel came out of the temple, crying with a loud voice to Him who sat on the cloud, 'Thrust in Your sickle and reap, for the time has come for You to reap, for

the harvest of the earth is ripe.' So He who sat on the cloud thrust in His sickle on the earth, and the earth was reaped."

In the midst of the fury of changes and challenges today, there is a wheat field of worship warriors, watchmen, rising from the grassroots of prayer in the nations. A spiritual awakening has begun. Years of sowing seeds of worship and prayer in ministry will most certainly move into a time of reaping the harvest. The bowls in heaven are tipping in favor of the saints. Now is the time when troubles, the "tares," and the body of Christ, the "wheat," are maturing together. There are distinct and difficult challenges almost everywhere you look. God is using these challenges to mature us, the body of Christ.

While on a missionary prayer journey to Mount Ararat, we spent a night at the base of the mountain near the Iranian border. The area felt incredibly oppressed, and the room we stayed in was heavy with secondary smoke. My chest felt like it was in a wine press. Trying to get a breath of fresh air, I opened the window. Though it was winter, the air was a welcome relief, and I spent the night shivering by an open window. Around 4 am, a most unusual sound awakened me. Outside I heard a flock of chirping birds fly by. The sound was distinct. The chirping continued, and another flock flew past. Wave after wave, "Spring-like" chirping birds flew by. How could there be birds in this cold, wintery place? The Lord quickened my heart that even in the darkest, most oppressed places of the earth, new hope is now rising. A shift is taking place. Get ready; a harvest is at hand! The earth is His and the fullness thereof. He has not forgotten nor forsaken and is ever watchful over His word to perform it.

Such are the times we live in today. Though pressed by challenging cultural pressures on every side, God is raising a remnant responding to the call of "Watchmen," in preparation for an end time harvest burgeoning at the door. They will be called and set in place, to foster, contend, and nurture the harvest into its fullness. The revival that ushers in the lost will be based on principles, not a program. Emphasized in these principles will be the foundations of the great commandments given in Matthew 22: 37-39, loving God and loving one another. Matthew 22:40 brands their impact with Jesus' words, "Upon these two commandments hang all the Law and the Prophets." Watchmen hear the sound of this end-time call and are beginning to connect across the nations. The values embraced by this movement can be applied in all cultures as they are from solid biblical foundations. Understanding the role of the watchman and the "Watch" is vital for the fullness of the Gentile church and impetus for this book. Those who are called to see and hear this message and the principles it reflects will be part of God's plan to usher the church into its finest hour. Behold the harvest is at hand. Watchmen rise and build!

Contents

One

Remnant Rising

"You shall keep watch of the house lest it be
broken down."

2 Kings 11:6

Living in a post 9/11 era, the specter of terrorism continues to dot the pages of headline news. The attacks of 09/11/2001 will forever be etched in the annals of world history. There is no doubt the violence and destruction of that day opened a distinct gateway of terrorism into the nations. The devastations catapulted to the headlines of the global news. No nation was untouched. The ramifications of the attacks continue to direct how we travel, relate, communicate, do business today.

Since 2001, however, there has been a distinct shift. Reaction to these events has changed. The news and brutality of terrorist activities are now so frequent people have become hardened to the travesty of these attacks. Softened world views have blurred the boundaries of "right" vs. "wrong." What once would have been a major "Red light," in society's moral view, now merely blink a pale "Yellow light" or in many cases incites no response at all.

The question now is, what are we going to do about the increasing lawlessness and violent times in which we live? What is the Holy Spirit saying to the church in response to the cultural decline and resistance ever before us? As a result of these challenges, God has the answer. A distinct "sound" has been released as He is calling forth "Watchmen" to join ranks across the nations. The call is inspiring urgency in the body of Christ, and subsequently, an underlying movement is underway. The impetus of this book is to explore this end-time directive, its biblical and prophetic history, characteristics, and its role. There is a distinct purpose unfolding for "Watchmen" in ushering in the end-time harvest and the Church into its finest hour. In preparation, it is worthwhile taking a look at an overview of some cultural shifts since 9/11/2001. These changes are markers for God's answers and give insight to this watchman call to the body of Christ today.

Reviewing some cultural indicators reflective of today, a recent study by the Barna Group relayed the fact that teens questioned viewed not recycling trash more immoral than viewing pornography.[1] Gang-related activity is moving out of inner cities to previously safe suburbs because of their smaller police departments. Alternative lifestyles have blurred core identity issues. Today, we as Christians, struggle to maintain a moral compass in cultures whose boundaries of right and wrong are increasingly blurred by social and political pressures.

Numerous studies have targeted various elements of society to evaluate cultural health. Common themes examined are state of marriage, industriousness, births to single mothers, religiosity. Studies show an increasing disparity leaving the working class "cut off from the richest sources of social capital: marriage, two-parent families, and

---

1 https://www.barna.com/research/teens-young-adults-use-porn-more-than-anyone-else/

church-going.[2]" In an article "Ten Signs of Culture's End," Brad Keena
outlines ten indicators of a culture's decline.[3] They are worth mention-
ing here as they signal the times in which we live. Though these are indicators focused on America, many of these indicators relate to Western
culture.

1) "The first sign of the end of a culture is that of a society which no
   longer worships or acknowledges God.
   a. Thanks to "Political Correctness," the popular culture ridicules
   those who worship God as the sovereign creator. Instead, it is
   popular to put our faith and trust in ourselves or other creations
   of God.
2) A second indicator of the end of a culture is the decline of the
   family.
   a. Today, statistics show divorce is at an all-time high in the United
   States. It is now so common for young people to grow up in
   divorced households that the term "broken family" is now a forgotten expression in the popular culture.
3) A third important indicator of cultural demise is society's low view
   of life.
   a. Popular culture now views abortion as a "right."
4) Another sign of the end of the civilization is the prevalence of base
   and immoral entertainment.
   a. In its last days, Rome had become a society with an insatiable
   appetite for debauchery and immorality. Perverted entertainment

2 http://www.realclearpolitics.com/articles/2011/04/12/coming_apart_at_the_
seams_109527.html
3 http://www.realclearpolitics.com/articles/2011/04/12/coming_apart_at_the_
seams_109527.html

translated into perverted speech and behavior. The Roman society began to accept and encourage open homosexuality. The people turned away from God and forgot his commandments and precepts, and Rome crumbled. And today our culture has begun to embrace the same.

5) Still, another troublesome indicator of society's demise is the increase in violent crime among young people.

   a. Riddled with gang violence, many of our inner cities have become powder kegs portending future collapse.

6) Another key cultural indicator is the declining middle class.

7) Yet another sign of cultural demise is that of an insolvent government.

8) Related to this, a government that lives off of society's moral decay is another sign of the end of civilization.

   a. The National Endowment for the Arts and the Legal Services Corporation are examples of agencies that foster society's decline. Within the judicial branch of government, judges accountable to no one have helped undermine the religious freedoms that were once the centerpiece of our society.

9) One obvious indicator that culture is in decline is when the ruling class loses its will.

   a. Politicians have discovered one of the keys to re-election is to advocate more spending and government programs for the poor. The traditional middle class is now defined as rich.

10) The final indicator of the demise of a civilization is the **failure of its people to see what is happening.**"

Such indicators of moral decline are well and active in present-day Western culture. The final indicator of the demise of people able to see and interpret what is happening is particularly alarming. Can we truly see what is happening in our culture?

Troubled by the level and severity of crime increasing, I asked a local city police officer if there was one single factor fueling it. His answer stunned me. He thought for a moment and said "The human heart…it has become increasingly dark." It is food for thought as we watch demonstrations and acts of rebellion unfurl defying values that fifty years ago would have been considered standard. What will "normal" everyday life be like in ten years if we continue in moral ambiguity?

As relayed early in this chapter, the focus of this book is not about the difficulties and the darkness of the day, but on an amazing plan and purpose of God unfolding. In this picture of cultural "hardness," and the reality of the harshness of the times, fields are being prepared for a powerful end-time harvest. The question is, do we see the fields? If we do, how do we respond? Are we ready to make the adjustments necessary to usher in this harvest? The pursuit of these questions is the visionary purpose of this book. In discovering their answers lies powerful truths hidden in God's Word that is emerging for such a time as this.

THE HARVEST:

Jesus saw the harvest before it happened. He chose the most unlikely of places, Samaria, and the most unlikely of people, a woman, a prostitute nonetheless, to save an entire city. It was here in this hard, despised place Jesus said, "Behold, I say to you, lift up your eyes and look at the fields, for they are already white for harvest!" John 4:35. In the hard, difficult places of our lives, the streets of our cities, and nations today, do we see the harvest before us? Jesus' parable of the wheat and the tares carries insightful and significant parallels for today:

"The kingdom of heaven is like a man who sowed good seed in his field; but while men slept, his enemy came and sowed tares among the wheat and went his way. But when the grain had sprouted and produced a crop, then the tares also appeared. So the servants of the owner came and said to him, 'Sir, did you not sow good seed in your field? How then does it have tares?' He said to them, 'An enemy has done this.' The servants said to him, 'Do you want us then to go and gather them up?' But he said, 'No, lest while you gather up the tares, you also uproot the wheat with them. Let both grow together until the harvest, and at the time of harvest I will say to the reapers, "First gather together the tares and bind them in bundles to burn them, but *gather the wheat into my barn.*"' Matthew 13:24-30

Early in the planting and growth of a wheat field, the wheat and tares cannot be differentiated. That is why Jesus cautions us not to pull out the tares in early stages of wheat field growth. Such action would damage wheat. They must grow together. Only when wheat and tares mature, can they be differentiated. The tares remain stiff, and upright, however mature wheat heads bend. What if God is using the growth and intensity of these modern day difficulties, tares, to mature us? The horrific reports of ISIS, and every act of violence, soaring crime rates, drugs, pornography and its repercussions, are present day tares maturing before our very eyes!

Today, the harvest of wheat and separation from the tares is happening at all levels. From personal levels to corporate levels, locally, nationally and internationally, the differentiation between wheat and tares is emerging. The contrast is becoming more and more defined. As the tares grow, we can be tested. God uses these times to mature us.

Countless times in my walk with the Lord, when I have been tested to the point of breaking, God has used it to humble me, to take me to that absolute point of surrender. In the process of giving up and giving in, the wheat within me became heavy and bent. It has been at these points of greatest stress, that God breaks the grip of the tares, and the wheat of revelation and wisdom unfolds its life within me. Without these tests, maturing would be difficult. Through life's challenges, James 1:2-3 does its work, "My brethren, count it all joy when you fall into various trials, knowing that the testing of your faith produces patience. But let patience have its perfect work, that you may be perfect and complete, lacking nothing."

In a chance encounter at a community outreach center, a few of us gathered to review it for a "Revive" night of worship. Amongst those gathered was a man who had obviously taken the trip on drugs and journeyed to his last "leg" in life. During the conversation, he left and went into the small sanctuary. When he did not return, I left the group and followed him into the room. When I opened the door, I was stunned. The man had picked up a guitar and started strumming and humming a tune. The Presence of the Lord and anointing was strong. A few others came in and abruptly stopped at the door. We were all speechless by what we saw and heard.

A little while later, when we were out on the street again, we had the boldness to talk and pray with him. There on the city streets, the man crumpled in tears as words of life renewed hope in him. Truth began to dispel the grip of darkness. The following Sunday at church, there was an altar call for new believers. I happened to turn around and there behind me was this homeless man, raising his hand vigorously. That night, baptisms were offered for new believers. Yes, he was one who went forward. Not only did he get baptized but he received the gift of tongues as a manifestation of God's Spirit upon him. This man's story is an example of the harvest. Over the course of a few short days, a few encouraging words, and an encounter with the living God, the wheat within this man was harvested and the grip of the tares released.

On a broader level, larger harvest fields are looming globally. We are living in a time when the sheep and the goat nations will become increasingly identified and clear. The harvest will be critical in releasing the identity of these nations. In fact, the tares are so strong in some places the underlying wheat field is difficult to see. But Jesus saw the harvest before others could see it. Today, what do we see? Out of the persecution and terrors of the times, a diaspora of now almost 60 million refugees is being driven out of otherwise difficult countries to reach. 4.4 million alone have come out of Syria to our doorsteps. Do we see the harvest being sent to us? What if those from Syria and surrounding nations are being released to hear the gospel? Reports are being released that many refugees are disenfranchised with Islam.[4] Encountering a loving church, the alienated are hearing the joyful and loving good news of salvation through Jesus and receiving it. On fire for the Lord, many are being called to go back to make a difference in their country. What if God is sending the harvest to us to be sown back into these nations to fulfill Isaiah 19:25 destiny for Assyria to be the "work of His hands." The import of these nations is outlined in Revelation 21:9-16 describing the New Jerusalem. A process for the restoration of these nations may very well be at hand in preparation for Jesus' return.

Within the distresses of the immigrant crises, the gangs, drug abusers, and homeless on our streets, a harvest is waiting. Even within the western church, tares of complacency and religious tradition threaten to choke the life and vitality out of the wheat in its midst. But God is using it all to prepare hearts to receive the full salvation and reality of Christ within, the hope of glory. Tired of religious ideology, violence, manipulation, control, and deception that threaten core life values, wheat is now ready, more than ever, to receive the fullness and reality of God's love, grace, and mercy. The real news behind the difficulties today is the heralding sound of the harvest!

---

4 https://www.opendoorsusa.org/christian-persecution/stories/muslims-turn-to-christ-in-unprecedented-numbers-pt-1/

The clarion call now is to *"Gather the wheat into the barn!"* Matthew 13:30. The signs are upon us.

REMNANT RISING:

One of the key biblical roles of Watchmen (the word encompasses both men and women throughout this book) was to be stationed in ramparts to watch the fields as the harvesters brought in the produce. The role of watchmen was very significant in the agrarian culture of the day. Guarding the fields against animals and thieves, was vital to the community. Similarly, a spiritual harvest is at hand. God is calling watchmen to build the spiritual ramparts, the culture of prayer, to pray in and watch over the harvest at hand. A remnant is rising awakened to the urgency of the hour. They are discerning and skilled in separating the wheat from the tares. Skilled in the Word, they also carry the strength and humility required to build with others. They are willing to contend for the full redemptive call of God for their lives, families, cities, and nations.

Watchmen today are building where walls have gaps or have fallen. They function through committed prayer and ongoing communication to create community through relationships. As walls between ramparts are mended or connected, communication and relationships form foundations for effective battle strategies to protect and defend God's harvest. Historic outpourings of God's Spirit such as the Knights of St. John, Herrnhut, Germany, that lasted more than a few years, all had "Watchmen" mobilized and in place.

Over the years of responding to the call to "Watch," we have distinctly underestimated the power of its role in our personal lives and to the body of Christ. We have also distinctly underestimated the enemy assignment against it. Jesus knew what He was saying when He exhorted the disciples during His final hours on earth, "Could you not watch with me one hour?" Matthew 26:40; Mark 14:37. He knew the single most powerful history making event was about to take place and called the disciples into their God-given role on earth…to "Watch."

We are in similar times today. God is awakening the church for another powerful history making event, Jesus' return to rule and reign. Much of what we face today is the result of Watchmen not being on the wall or effectively connected. The rise of terrorism, moral decay, crime, drugs, and abuse are evidence of lack of watching. Ezekiel 33:1-7 is a sobering word and is playing out before our eyes:

> "Again the word of the Lord came to me, saying, 'Son of man, speak to the children of your people, and say to them: 'When I bring the sword upon a land, and the people of the land take a man from their territory and make him their watchman, when he sees the sword coming upon the land, if he blows the trumpet and warns the people, then whoever hears the sound of the trumpet and does not take warning, if the sword comes and takes him away, his blood shall be on his own head. He heard the sound of the trumpet, but did not take warning; his blood shall be upon himself. But he who takes warning will save his life. But if the watchman sees the sword coming and does not blow the trumpet, and the people are not warned, and the sword comes and takes any person from among them, he is taken away in his iniquity; but his blood I will require at the watchman's hand.' 'So you, son of man: I have made you a watchman for the house of Israel; therefore you shall hear a word from My mouth and warn them for Me.'"

When the tares of terrorism strike or moral decay raise its agenda against the righteous, our question should now be "Where are the watchmen?"

The trumpet is sounding now for the "Watchmen" to rise and build. God is moving to redeem and restore, to separate the wheat and the tares for an end-time harvest. Are we prepared? Through investigating and exploring the biblical foundations, functional roles and characteristics of a watch and watchman today, our prayer is that this book will equip, prepare and open our eyes to the import and impact of the watchman. It is a call to and for the Church moving into its finest hour.

APPLICATIONS:

1) What "Tares," personal and cultural, do you see influencing your life today?
2) How have personal difficulties influenced your relationships?
3) How have the cultural "tares" impacted the church today?
4) What is God's scriptural response?

Two

THE JOURNEY

"Surely the Lord God does nothing unless He
reveals His secret to His servants the prophets."

Amos 3:7

When my husband and I first met, we were both in the trenches of
medical school. We were both sincere but young believers. I was
drawn to him in the medical school lounge studying with a Bible at the
edge of his desk. Somehow, I garnered the boldness during a break to just
say "Hello." The introduction proved to be the door for continued relationship. As I had dedicated myself to a four year Bible study, Fred agreeably
joined me. We got our feet planted in the Word of God as we journeyed
through the rigors of medical school and the training required. It was
preparing us for what was to come.

As we launched out in early family life, looking in from the outside, one
would have more than likely considered us faithful Christians. However, as
dedicated and sincere as we were, we knew something was missing. It wasn't
until our youngest son was born that we became convicted of our prayerless-
ness through the work of Larry Lea and his book, <u>Could you not Tarry One</u>

Hour.[5] We became so convicted of our lack of real relationship and intimacy with God that we decided to do just what Jesus said. We dedicated an hour a day in prayer. Usually, it was the early morning hours. Fred would take our youngest son on a prayer drive, and I would have peace and quiet with the Lord for an hour at home. We would then come back share what the Lord had spoken. That single decision and discipline to carry out the commitment to pray changed our lives. It was preparing us for the storm to come.

No sooner had we dropped to our knees when everything around us began to shake. Without going into a long tirade of events, God shook us to the core of our being. Everything that could be shaken was shaken, from jobs, home, finances, to health. He made sure we stayed on our knees. We went through a season of testing that, in retrospect, was training for what we are being called to do today.

We didn't know it at the time, but during these tumultuous years, in the months between 1999-2000 in the trenches of the prayer movement, God blew upon the earth an extraordinary end-time plan. Amos 3:7 states, "Surely the Lord God does nothing unless He reveals His secret to His servants the prophets." God spoke His desire for 24/7 prayer to three servants, Dick Eastman, Mike Bickle, and Peter Grieg all on approximately the same September day virtually unbeknownst to each other. Additionally, in June 2000, the Lord also spoke to Graham Power, from Cape Town, South Africa, about uniting the body of Christ through the vision and mobilization of a Global Day of Prayer.

These extraordinary encounters mobilized an awakening in prayer, a "Watchman Call," throughout the globe fueling much of what we are experiencing today. With supernatural favor, these moves of prayer arose

---

5 Lea, Larry, Could you Not Tarry One Hour, Charisma House, 1999.

so that when 2000 rolled into place, a dynamic force of prayer had begun to emerge from multiple places. Before 1999, if you asked people about a house of prayer, a prayer room, or prayer ministry you would likely be met with a blank face. But after 1999, the terms increasingly became a motivational force and common terminology for many.

The events 09/11/2001 and the coordinated attacks in New York City, Pennsylvania, and Washington, DC, reinforced the prayer/worship mobilization underway and accentuated the need for united corporate prayer. Though parts of the movement of worship and prayer responded, the desperation and concern 09/11 incited died within a few months. However, a distinct spiritual gate of terrorism was opened, and its seeds were cast across the earth. These seeds, tares, would continue to grow to fuel the difficulties we face today.

A VISION AND PROPHETIC JOURNEY:

During this time of intense spiritual activity and warfare, in October 2000, I had a vision, an open vision. The Lord took me to the streets of New York where suddenly two towers exploded in front of me. The building collapsed in a giant heap of cement and steel frames. All of a sudden, a giant pair of hands came out of the sky and scooped up the rubble. The hands kneaded the rubble like clay. When they opened, I saw an enormous clock tower. The clock tower was the image of Big Ben.

The vision was particularly alarming for two reasons. First of all, it was very clear. Secondly, there was a distinct paradigm shift in the atmosphere as the warfare broke and the peace of God settled in. My bewildered, broken and contrite heart was not despised as the healing balm of God's Presence flooded my body, soul, and spirit. A dramatic shift had taken place, and a journey into progressive revelation began to unfold. I rose from my knees rubbing my eyes in bewilderment with a new heart hungry to know more. Within a couple of weeks, I was healed, and back to normal.

In seeking the Lord for the understanding, I heard "Athaliah at the gates." Athaliah means, "afflicted of the Lord.[6]" Athaliah was the daughter of Ahab and Jezebel. She ruled Israel with a reign of terror. She killed the children of inheritance and usurped the throne from the rightful heirs. Her rule hindered true seed from coming to full fruition. She stole the rightful inheritance from those God had ordained. She usurped God-given authority and aborted spiritual babies preventing them from coming into maturity. Her rule, however, collapsed as those who carried and understood covenant, the priests, organized "Watches" at key gates of the city. As they did so, they stood to watch over the promised inheritance.

"In the seventh year Jehoiada sent and brought the captains of hundreds—of the body guards and the escorts and brought them into the house of the Lord....he commanded them saying, 'This is what you shall do: One-third of you who come on duty on the Sabbath shall be keeping watch over the king's house, one-third shall be at the gate of Sur, and one-third at the gate behind the escorts. You shall keep watch of the house, lest it be broken down," 2 Kings 11:4-6

I knew something devastating was going to happen to the country and the "Watch" would be very instrumental in its deliverance.

Ten months later we received an early morning phone call. A voice on the other line cried out, "Turn on the television!" It was a friend of mine who knew of the open vision. Immediately I went to the TV and was riveted, as was my husband, Fred. The scene being broadcast on TV was the mirror image of what I had seen ten months earlier in the open vision. We

---

6 Strong's h6271 Atalya

knew then the Lord had shown us something. Watching the events unfold, we were thrust into a battle for our hearts and minds that shattered our paradigm of thinking. Furthermore, the date of 9/11 had significant meaning in our family, on both sides. Knowing the impact of the open vision just ten months earlier, we ran into the throne room desperately seeking God's directives. We knew something BIG had just happened, and God was drawing our attention to it and to Him.

As we have traversed various phases of the "Watch" in our region, the Lord began to speak to our hearts about a "Global Watch." Big Ben, from the open vision, is an icon of World Time. The attacks of 9/11 impacted world history. The open vision was not just about 09/11/2001, it was about something in the future, and it carried global weight....a Global Watch.

Just as it was in the time of Jehoiada and Jehosheba, God is now preparing a time for the true King, Jesus Christ, to be revealed. In preparation, He is inspiring the watchmen to rise and build. We are in times when the wheat and the tares are both maturing together as the earth is being prepared for a great end-time harvest. Watchmen are being stationed to usher in and protect the harvest.

"The kingdom of heaven is like a man who sowed good seed in his field; but while men slept, his enemy came and sowed tares among the wheat and went his way. But when the grain had sprouted and produced a crop, then the tares also appeared. So the servants of the owner came and said to him, 'Sir, did you not sow good seed in your field? How then does it have tares?' He said to them, 'An enemy has done this.' The servants said to him, 'Do you want us then to go and gather them up?' But he said, 'No, lest while you gather up the tares, you also uproot the wheat with them. Let both grow together until the harvest, and at the time of harvest I will say to the reapers, 'First gather together the tares and bind them in bundles to burn them, but gather the wheat into my barn.'" Matthew 13:24-30

As persecution, judgments, devastations shake the earth, everything that can be shaken will be shaken in preparation for His return. Watchmen are being called to build their ramparts, their communities, and connect across the globe to prepare the way for His return. For out of the turmoil, a harvest is coming, and an alert, ready and watchful bride is emerging.

The years of carrying the vision have been punctuated by God's supernatural hand intervening to bring confirmations, revelation, understanding and the very things necessary for an entity such as a Global Watch to manifest.

PROPHETIC CONVERGENCE, CONFIRMATION, AND MESSAGE:

We later found out that the scriptures spoken in synagogues around the world on 09/11/2001 were Isaiah 61:10-63:09.[7] Isaiah 62:6 prophecies the raising up of Watchmen that will be posted on the walls of Jerusalem… "they shall not keep silent day or night." Isaiah 63:1-6 prophecies of the rise of ISIS and what God will do. Though hidden by the emphasis on the attacks by news media that day, the redemptive call of God behind the scenes was ushered into the world through the Jewish people! The passages were a riveting prophetic message from God to the nations of the earth for His redemptive plan. These scriptures convey one of the clearest calls for the "Watch" in the entire Bible and sound a clarion call to the nations.

"I have set watchmen on your walls O Jerusalem; they shall never hold their peace day or night, You who make mention of the Lord

---

7 http://www.hebcal.com/sedrot/nitzavim

do not keep silent and give Him no rest till He establishes and till He makes Jerusalem a praise in the earth." Isaiah 62:6-7.

Interestingly, as a prophetic picture of ISIS, Isaiah 63 relays God's judgment, v. 1-6; and His call for those who would stand in the gap, v.5; intertwined with His mercy, v. 4, 7-9.

"Who is this who comes from Edom, with dyed garments from Bozrah, This One who is glorious in His apparel, traveling in the greatness of His strength?—'I who speak in righteousness, mighty to save.' Why is Your apparel red, and Your garments like one who treads in the winepress? 'I have trodden the winepress alone, and from the peoples, no one was with Me. For I have trodden them in My anger, and trampled them in My fury; their blood is sprinkled upon My garments, and I have stained all My robes. For the day of vengeance is in My heart, and the year of My redeemed has come. I looked, but there was no one to help, and I wondered that there was no one to uphold; therefore My own arm brought salvation for Me; and My own fury, it sustained Me. I have trodden down the peoples in My anger, made them drunk in My fury, And brought down their strength to the earth.'" Isaiah 63:1-6

The prophetic call for Watchmen and the warning of devastations to come converging in these scriptures on such a historic day is fearfully accurate. It reflects a holy God, "Watching over My word to perform it," Jeremiah 1:13. The birth pangs and blood on the streets are now impacting all nations. We do not know when the next terrorist strike will be. The call for the Watchmen is real. They understand the appeal made by Ephesians 6:12-13:

"For we do not wrestle against flesh and blood, but against principalities, against powers, against the rulers of the darkness of this age, against spiritual hosts of wickedness in the heavenly places. Therefore take up the whole armor of God, that you may be able to withstand in the evil day, and having done all, to stand."

FROM WATCHMAN CALL TO WATCHMAN RESPONSE:

Though far from complete, these historic and prophetic insights over the past several decades are marks and stamps of God's confirmation and call to the watchmen. As times have intensified and accelerated, we are now in the process of shifting from the "Watchman Call" to the "Watchman Response." Due to the urgency of the hour, watchmen are now being called to work together. Not only are they positioned (called) to their rampart (community), but are now searching to connect with others in response to the times. Those awakened to the challenges of today realize the battle cannot be fought separated on the wall.

Much like in Nehemiah's time, the various "families" are joining in constructing their part of the wall for they have a "mind to work," Nehemiah 4:6. Nehemiah "Set the people according to their families, with their swords, their spears, and their bows," Nehemiah 4:13. In other words, each of the families, participants, carried their ministry calling and gifting and used it to build the wall, side by side, with other families. No one lost their identity, ministry, call, leadership structure while laboring in construction. Rather all were strengthened and helped. Eventually, "Those who built on the wall, and those who carried burdens, loaded themselves so that with one hand they worked at construction, and with the other held a weapon," Nehemiah 4:17. True watchmen function to encourage growth and defend the wall from enemy attacks. Nehemiah 4:19-20 explains the role of a watch,

"The work is great and extensive and we are separated far from one another on the wall. Wherever you hear the sound of the trumpet, rally to us there. Our God will fight for us."

Subsequently, as the wall was built, an entire city was reconstructed, revival and reformation followed. Today the function of a watch carries a similar weight. There is transformational power when it is in place.

We are living in extraordinary times. The call to those who would take their place as Watchmen is resounding across the nations. Through the turmoil, upheaval, and shakings in the nations, God's light is becoming stronger and heralding the watchmen to take their place on the wall. Just as in the times of 2 Kings 11, God is raising up the watches, to stand guard in their assigned place. Though this summary just scratches the surface of "The Journey," we pray it inspires your hearts to respond to the call of God. Run with the vision. It shall tarry no more (Habakkuk 2:1-3). The time is now. The body is becoming the bride, awakened, ready and alert! The true King is coming. The Watch will prepare the way for His rule and reign!

APPLICATION

1. What were the circumstances around you when you first came to know the Lord?
2. Did the circumstances say anything about God's call on your life?
3. Review the strategic points in time when you have encountered God in a significant way. Was there a message in it for you, for your call in life?

Three

THE STANCE: BIBLICAL FOUNDATIONS

"Then the Lord God took the man and put him
in the garden of Eden to tend and keep it."

Genesis 2:15

As God moves to awaken the church in the acceleration of the times, what characterizes the role of a watchman? Are there distinguishing marks? How does the role differ from any other prayer ministry? The terms "watch" and "watchman" are not new. The concept of the role flows throughout the Old and New Testament. A central call for its function is stated in Habakkuk 2:1, "I will stand my watch and set myself on the rampart, and watch to see what He will say to me." No matter what function the watchman carried, whether to stand on the city wall, oversee the harvest, walk the city streets, there are consistent biblical themes that help identify the role today. We are in times when God is raising up those who will "Watch," to fulfill scripture's exhortations, "Watch, therefore, for you know neither the day nor the hour in which the Son of Man is coming," Matthew 25:13.

BIBLICAL CALL:

Tom Hess in His book, <u>The Watchman,</u> states that all are called to be a watch-man.[8] If that is the case, how do we identify with its role and ministry? We understand the five-fold ministry and its import, but what about the "watch-man?" What does that mean? What role does the watchman play in the body of Christ? The best description and foundational call for a "Watchman" comes right from the Word itself. In the beginning, "God created man in Our image, according to Our likeness," Genesis 1:26. Genesis 2:15 describes man's pur-pose, "Then the Lord God took the man and put him in the garden of Eden to tend and keep it." "Tend" is the Hebrew word "abad," meaning to serve, or execute, husbandman. The word "keep" is the word "samar" or in some translations, "shamar," meaning guard/defend, preserve, or "watch." In other words, God's intended purpose for mankind is to "serve and watch or defend," the garden He has given us. We are all called to be watchmen. Failure to do so has led to many of the destructive forces we now face on Earth.

What is the essence of the word "Abad" to tend? Through the various scriptural references, the word "Abad" appears most commonly in asso-ciation with tending fields, tilling ground (Genesis 3:23, 4:12), or where we spend our time working (Exodus 5:18); or in serving (Exodus 4:23). Numbers 3:8 relays the fundamental nature of abad, "Also they shall attend to all the furnishings of the tabernacle of meeting, and to the needs of the children of Israel, to *do* the work of the tabernacle." In the New Testament, 1 Corinthians 3:16 states that we are the temple of God, "Do you not know that you are the temple of God and that the Spirit of God dwells in you?" Our relationship with Jesus reflects the "Abad," the taking care of our temple, in the New Testament. Jesus expresses the essence of "Abad" in the New Testament in John 15:15-16, "No longer do I call you servants,

---

8 Hess, Tom, <u>The Watchman</u>, Morningstar Pub., 96, pg 11.

for a servant, does not know what his master is doing; but I have called you friends, for all things that I heard from My Father I have made known to you," John 15:15-16. Friends spend time, share and are willing to serve each other. Such is the stance of the watchman. It is a type of walk that moves us from being "for Him" to "being with Him" so that we can see and discern accurately and know how to serve and grow the garden He has given us.

If "Abad" is to tend, what does "Samar," guard, watch, protect? Throughout scripture, the Hebrew word *samar* is associated with God's covenant and intended blessing for mankind:

- Genesis 2:15 "To tend and *keep* the garden God gave them."
- Genesis 17:9 "As for you, you shall *keep* My covenant, you and your descendants after you throughout their generations. This is My covenant which you shall keep, between Me and you and your descendants after you."
- Exodus 12:24: "And you shall *observe* this thing as an ordinance for you and your sons forever."
- Exodus 13:10 "You shall therefore *keep* this ordinance (Passover) in its season from year to year."
- Leviticus 18:4 "You shall *observe* My judgments and keep My ordinances to walk in them."
- Leviticus 18:26 "You shall therefore *keep* My statutes and My judgments."
- Leviticus 18:30 "Therefore you shall *keep* My ordinance."
- Proverbs 4:4-6 "He also taught me and said to me: 'Let your heart retain my words; *Keep* my commands and live.'"

From the verses above, God commands us to "Samar," to watch over, to guard and defend His covenant, His ordinances, His statutes. This kind of attentiveness is a mighty responsibility and call of God! Why? Jesus warns of the end-times in Matthew 24:4-17:

"Take heed that no one deceives you. For many will come in My name, saying, 'I am the Christ,' and will deceive many. And you will hear of wars and rumors of wars. See that you are not troubled; for all these things must come to pass, but the end is not yet. For nation will rise against nation, and kingdom against kingdom. And there will be famines, pestilences, and earthquakes in various places. All these are the beginning of sorrows.

Then they will deliver you up to tribulation and kill you, and you will be hated by all nations for My name's sake. And then many will be offended, will betray one another, and will hate one another. Then many false prophets will rise up and deceive many. And because lawlessness will abound, the love of many will grow cold."

These are chilling thoughts and reflective of life today. As such, God is looking for those who will take the stance as "Watchman." He is looking for those who will guard and protect His word and purposes…those who will "climb the ramparts to see what He will say to them," Habakkuk 2:1. The role and function carry the weight and responsibility in caring for and defending His covenant plan and purpose in our lives! "Samar" is a powerful call of God to mankind to protect His purpose for life itself in the face of increasing opposition and deception.

BIBLICAL CHARACTERISTICS:

Though we are all called to "Watch," not everyone picks up the role or develops the mandate to watch over the "fields" God has given them.

Though the call of the watchman is core to God's purpose in our lives, it is our answer to that call that develops the character.

What are common characteristics in people who answer the call to "Watch?" These traits weave throughout the course of the Bible. All the traits indicate an underlying walk of a worship/warrior carrying deep intimacy with the Lord.

Prophetic Gifting: There are three dimensions of the watchman that undergird the mandate to "Tend and keep" their garden, the burden, or ministry call they have been given. These characteristics are to see, hear, and declare and are reflective of their prophetic gifting or nature.

- See: "I will stand my watch, and set myself on the rampart and watch to see what He will say to me," Habakkuk 2:1.
- Hear: "Son of man, I have made you a watchman for the house of Israel; therefore hear a word from My mouth, and give them warning from Me." Ezekiel 3:17
- Declare: "Go set a watchman, let him declare what he sees." Isaiah 21;6

Throughout scripture, watchmen demonstrated these prophetic characteristics to influence God's people. More will be discussed in the coming chapters.

Perseverance: Watchmen persevere in the burdens, the assignments God has given them. Isaiah 62:5 says that they "shall never hold their peace day or night. You who make mention of the Lord, do not keep silent." Though difficulties may arise, watchmen learn to persevere through the challenges life presents. Jeremiah wept bitterly over a nation facing judgment that would not listen to the Lord. Jeremiah 44:16 states, "As for the word that you have spoken to us in the name of the Lord, we will not listen to you." Ezekiel, a watchman to a demoralized remnant of Judah exiled in Babylon, persevered in the face of much rejection. The Lord explained, "But the house of Israel will not listen to you because they will not listen to Me," Ezekiel 3:7. Sounds like a joyful, warm, loving place to be! We will investigate further this quality in the chapter "Relentless." Suffice it to say; watchmen know and cultivate the character to run the race with endurance so as to receive the prize, 1 Corinthians 9:24.

Discernment: Because of their close relationship with the Lord, watchmen will develop keen insight and foresight. Such a role is reflected in Habakkuk 2:1. They will "See" or discern what God is saying. Like the sons of Issachar, they have "understanding of the times, to know what Israel ought to do," 1 Chronicles 12:32. Today, the role of watchmen will often function to open spiritual eyes to what people or ministries ought to do to move forward or will frequently have answers to various difficulties or trials people face.

Faithfulness: "Without faith it is impossible to please Him," Hebrews Hebrews 11:6. It is through faith, watchmen hold their stance and perse-vere through the various challenges presented them. Given difficult and strenuous circumstances, watchmen know who and what to trust. Though they may grow weary, their faith keeps them in a place of continued peace. Psalm 9:10 declares, "And those who know Your name will put their trust in You; For You, Lord, have not forsaken those who seek You." Being dili-gent in seeking the Lord, watchmen find Him and stand in a position of faith that does not relent or give up.

Strong builders: Watchmen today have learned and walk out the value of collaboration and cooperation. One of the key distinctives of watchmen is that they are strong builders. 1 Peter 2:5 expresses the concept of build-ing well, "You also, as living stones, are being built up a spiritual house, a holy priesthood, to offer up spiritual sacrifices acceptable to God through

Jesus Christ," Watchmen know the import of working through relationships both in and between ministries. Understanding how to honor all involved in being called in or being called out of ministry is vital in the building process, lest the "wall be broken down." Watchmen truly understand these dynamics and work through change to build, and not tear down. More will be discussed in the chapter on "Stir and Spur Life."

BIBLICAL ROLES:
Though we have all been called to "Tend and keep" the garden God has given us, there are varied expressions, as to how this function is carried out. Biblically, God uses watchmen at strategic times to guard and protect His purpose. The purpose to "Serve and defend" God's covenant purpose is interwoven throughout these biblical roles.

Watchmen are strategic in God's plans to change the course of a nation. God used watchmen when the uprising of Absalom threatened the throne of David. "And the watchman went up to the roof over the gate, to the wall, lifted his eyes and looked," 2 Samuel 18 24. At the time of the overthrow of Jezebel, God used watchmen to bring victory for His purpose, 2 Kings 9:17-20. When Athaliah threatened to kill all those in line to inherit David's throne, watchmen were used to protect young Joash and subsequently the line of David that would lead to Jesus. 2 Kings 11:6 relays the call, "You shall keep watch of the house, lest it be broken down." Today, nations are being shaken. Alignments and political upheavals are happening and in the making. The sheep and goat nations are becoming more evident.

Now is the time, God is raising up watchmen from city to city, nation to nation to contend for their redemptive call. Their eyes look beyond the natural into what God has spoken. They are called to declare His promise and purpose as end-time prophetic fulfillment draws near.

Watchmen are used in protecting the purposes of God in a city. Typically, watchmen were posted on city walls where they functioned as sentries. Isaiah 21:8 states, "O Lord, I stand continually by day on the watchtower, and I am stationed every night at my guard post." An example of watchmen being key in protecting, restoring and transforming cities is in the book of Nehemiah. The strategy to build the walls required families of Israelites to work together. As they labored, the wall was built, the city was protected, and revival broke out. Watchman and their call to relentless prayer are vital components for revival culture to be sustained and maintained. Their role will be further discussed in the ensuing chapters. The spiritual hunger produced when watchmen prayer cultures arise in cities are significant signs of coming transformation and revival. Luke 12:37 promises,

> "Blessed are those servants whom the master when he comes, will find watching. Assuredly, I say to you that he will gird himself and have them sit down to eat, and will come in and serve them. And if he should come in the second watch, or come in the third watch, and find them so, blessed are those servants."

Watchmen are used in turning people back to the Lord. Particularly in times of imminent judgment, God used Watchmen not only to warn but exhort people to turn back to the Lord. Isaiah proclaimed during the fall of Babylon, "Go, set a watchman, let him declare what he sees," Isaiah 21:6. Furthermore, in Isaiah 21:12, "The watchman said, 'The morning comes, and also the night. If you will inquire, inquire; return! Come back!'" As spiritual "seers," Watchmen are used to warn but also exhort people of God's purposes. It may not be a popular stance. The life of Jeremiah and

Isaiah reflect the difficulties they faced. The words of their books are filled with exhortations to nations gone astray. Jeremiah 29:11-12 contains both the popular promise, "For I know the thoughts that I think toward you, says the Lord, thoughts of peace and not of evil, to give you a future and a hope," and exhortation, "And you will seek Me and find Me, when you search for Me with all your heart. I will be found by you, says the Lord, and I will bring you back from your captivity...where I have driven you, says the Lord," Jeremiah 29:13-14. Unfortunately, later Jeremiah declares, "I have driven them, because they have not heeded My words, says the Lord, which I sent to them by My servants the prophets," Jeremiah 29:18-19. Today, watchmen are being called in a similar fashion to not only declare the hope of the Lord but to exhort us to turn back to the Lord in increasingly dark days.

God raises watchmen at harvest times. Watchmen were placed in fields to keep watch over the crops guarding their fields against animals and thieves. Today, their towers are still in place in many places throughout Israel. It is a physical example of the spiritual counterpart of watchmen. As end-time prophecies are unfolding at an increasingly rapid rate, God is now raising up watchmen globally to build spiritual ramparts, communities of prayer, to prepare for His return. Jesus described the spiritual harvest we are entering in the parable of the wheat and the tares, "Let both grow together until the harvest, and at the time of harvest I will say to the reapers, 'First gather together the tares and bind them in bundles to burn them but gather the wheat into my barn,'" Matthew 13:30.

Watchmen are being positioned to hear, see, and herald the times and to steward the burgeoning spiritual harvest into the barn before His return. The process has begun. The trumpet is sounding, and watchmen are heeding the call.

THE FINISHING TOUCH:

One of the most compelling stories relaying the impact and import of Watchmen in the Bible is the story of Ruth. The entire book is a reflection of Watchmen walking out their redemptive roles. After the death of their husbands, Ruth was not willing to leave Naomi's, her mother-in-law's, side. Forsaking her pagan heritage, she chose to continue to care for the "garden," the family, that had been given her through marriage. Leaving all she knew as familiar, she followed Naomi back to Bethlehem. There, Boaz, a relative of Naomi's husband, was guarding and watching over his fields. Ruth wisely followed her mother-in-law's instructions to glean from the field being watched by Boaz. He noticed a foreigner in their midst picking the leftovers from the harvest. There in the middle of a field, interactions between family and cultures, servants, watchmen, and city gatekeepers all intertwined. Humility characterized every varied and necessary interaction in the story. Between Ruth and Naomi, Ruth and Boaz, Boaz and city leaders, Boaz to Naomi, each character treated each other with utmost respect and honor. No one was defiled, defamed or disrespected. No position was deposed. No culture was defamed. The fields each person was called to tend and keep were well taken care of. As humility permeated every interaction, each came into new strength, including Naomi who had endured much hardship only to finally go back to Israel, find and redeem her life. In the end, the story reflects the strength of women through Ruth, the valor of men in Boaz, and the glory of the children. It is a beautiful representation of how vigilant "watchfulness" over our lives prospers the Kingdom. As each of the figures, particularly Ruth and Boaz, stood to watch over their inheritance, the Lord made way for the savior of the world to be born.

APPLICATION:

1. What are the things in your life God has called you to "Tend and keep?" List and prioritize them.
2. What characteristics discussed (prophecy, perseverance, discernment, faithfulness, collaboration) are your strengths. Define areas that need working and what you could do to facilitate your personal growth.
3. What is the greatest challenge, or fear you face in collaborating with others in the body of Christ? (examples fear of losing control, fear of criticism)

Four

The Knock at the Door and the Call

"The work is great and extensive, and we are
separated far from
one another on the wall. Wherever you hear the
sound of the trumpet, rally to us there. Our God
will fight for us."

Nehemiah 4:19-20

It was a beautiful May evening. We had just come home from a conference we held in our city. The Presence of the Lord had been strong in
the meeting and was palpable in our home as we basked in the "afterglow."
The meeting had gone above and beyond our expectations. Signs followed
with wonderful testimonies of healings, and tremendous joy in those that
came. The Holy Spirit ministered deeply to the attendees, beyond what
we could measure. Yet, there was a yearning in our hearts. Something was
missing.

As we pondered what had just happened, suddenly there came loud
knock at the door. We went to the door and opened it. No one was there

but the pitch dark of a late Spring evening. There was no sound. We looked down the street and around the corner. There was no one to be seen. Suddenly my husband and I heard the same words, "There is no vessel that can contain My glory." We both looked at each other stunned by the words. Suddenly, the yearning in our hearts shifted into clarity as we sensed the meaning of God's words. Revelation filled a void in our hearts. We realized we had witnessed the value and power of the corporate body, but the vessel had vanished as people left to go back to their homes. In a few short but powerful words, the encounter changed the course and direction of our lives and ministry. We realized God was calling us to the needed development of the 2nd great commandment to fulfill our corporate experience, to love one another. Jesus spoke of it in Matthew 22:39, "And the second is like it: 'You shall love your neighbor as yourself.'"

The sudden reality of the need for stronger relational strength within our experience in the body of Christ, churches, ministries, and in particular the prayer movement transformed our thinking that day. We had been diligent to pursue our prayer assignments, but the connection, interweaving and building one another up in a most holy faith, had been weak, if not non-existent. In fact, we had seen and experienced the pain in relationships strained at the very least, if not fractured by jealousies, envies, or worse yet presumptions that discolored others without understanding. These activities were happening with people regularly coming out of corporate prayer environments. Scriptures opened in a fresh new way to the reality and import of the "great" commandments to Him. The process to discover that "vessel" that could contain His glory required a foundational shift in our thinking. Our path in ministry was re-directed that day. The knock on the door was the "wake-up call, " and the quest began.

THE PERSONAL CALL:

What are the elements of a vessel that can sustain a habitation of His Presence? Since that knock on the door, the question inspired a God given hunger and pursuit within us. Through the journey, we have discovered there are both individual and corporate components. Events do draw people together and can mobilize vision. But what happens three, six, or even twelve months down the line after the initial excitement and agreement have passed? There is frequently a "fall off" when people simply don't show up, or other issues take our attention elsewhere. In an event-driven culture and society, commitment is a word that 's hard to promote or sustain

It is true; there is often a catalyst towards a surge in prayer. Desperation or inspiration can supply the spiritual vigor required. The sustaining catalyst, however, is a truth held in Scripture and reflected in history. Jesus, through the grueling scorn of crowds, rejection, brutal beatings, misunderstandings, and agonizing loss of support from His dearest disciples, endured it all for the call of God upon His life. Through His sacrifice, His house was birthed, and it would be a House of Prayer…a house that would forever have access to the "holiest of holies." As a result, today we have access to that throne room, "By a new and living way He consecrated for us, through the veil," Hebrews 10:20. That access is forever available. No one can take it away.

Similarly, such sacrifice, desire for the holy of holies birthed in a broken and contrite heart is the key to the door of the throne room. "The sacrifices of God are a broken spirit, a broken and a contrite heart—these, O God, You will not despise," Psalm 51:17. Ongoing sustainable prayer is not birthed in the head, or in good intentions, good ideas, or even anointed teaching and impartation. It is birthed in a broken and contrite heart. That is the start of the call and it does not depart, Romans 11:29. The call marks those whom God has given specific assignments. From these God given encounters, everything else flows. Isaiah 22:22-23 relays the concept:

> "The key of the house of David I will lay on his shoulder; so he shall open, and no one shall shut, and he shall shut, and no one shall open. I will fasten him as a peg in a secure place, and he will become a glorious throne to his father's house."

Nehemiah wept when he heard about the condition of the walls of Jerusalem and received the mandate to go back to repair them, Nehemiah 1:4. Jacob wrestled with God before he received his new name and mantle, Genesis 32:24. Josiah wept before he received the call to restore true worship in the temple and covenant with the Lord, 2 Chronicles 34:27.

When we first moved to the city we live in now, God called us to pray. The city is located in a valley. Having come out of tremendous upheaval, our hearts were already tenderized towards God's purposes. I remember driving over the mountains looking into the valley below. It was dusk, and the lights were just coming on. I was awestruck to see the lights form a cross between the city and main freeway. The Presence of God fell, and the call of God came clearly to pray. I wept all the way into the city. Our boys who were with me, all under the age of 9, were silent...most unusual for active strong-willed boys. One of them put his hand on my shoulder as we entered the place that would hold our future. Though the boys did not understand the impact, we all felt the weight of a future opening before us. During the ensuing six months, the Lord had me up 70-80% of the nights driving and weeping over the city. It was through that season of time that the door to God's call opened...it has never shut and has led me on the road that I am traversing today.

THE CORPORATE CALL:

Our individual walk is essential, but it is our corporate community and commitment to prayer that is distinctive of a "watch." Though "the prayers of the righteous avails much," James 5:16, it is the corporate expression that changes history. We cannot deny the impact of corporate prayer in community. From God's command to Israel to gather on His feasts, to the Upper Room, through revival history, it is the corporate community and commitment to prayer/worship that carries great spiritual weight. To be effective watchmen, we must be connected. If we sound the trumpet and there is no one to respond, how can we sound the alarm or make a difference?

Today, not only are large corporate entities, churches, and houses of prayer of value and influential but now God is breathing upon the grassroots, those whom He has hidden in cities, regions, mountains, valleys, deserts, villages of the world. The small home groups, the two by two's that have persisted and not relented in ceaseless prayer for their communities. The import of these "hidden ones," cannot be denied in the days we are now encountering. Knowing their culture and community, the grassroots are an important transformational vehicle God will use in the coming days. In fact, when God asked us to step out into the formation of a "Global Watch," He said, "There are generals in the fields, waiting for their marching orders." We are finding them. There are powerful, vigilant yet humble watchman waiting for such a time as this to join ranks and build.

As grassroots prayer groups emerge, the fuel that continues to feed the engine is His Presence. To meet regularly, or to develop 24/7 prayer is not the goal. The goal is His Presence abiding in a vessel that seeks Him and commits to pray. James 4:8 says, "Draw near to God and He will draw near to you." Revival history confirms the import and impact of these committed corporate prayer and worship expressions.

In New York, the Fulton Street revival began with six people concerned for the lack of regard for God in a nation burgeoning and blossoming in prosperity were called to pray. On September 23, 1857, they met for the first time in a small rented space on Fulton Street in New York. Meeting weekly, the numbers began to climb. Then on October 10th, the Stock Market crashed. The dynamic success of the economy collapsed. The panic that ensued shifted the heart of America into what is known as the "Second Great Awakening." The small, not so insignificant prayer meeting blossomed from once a week to daily with up to 50,000 businessmen in attendance. By 1858, the prayer movement leapt to every major city in America and the Second Great Awakening erupted.

Many prayer ministries or churches have their vision, their vertical call, and governmental order in place. As committed believers align vertically with their ministry purpose, a watch supplies the horizontal connection. Within the horizontal connection is the fulfillment of the great commandments, upon which are all the "Law and the prophets," Matthew 22:40. Furthermore, the wheels of Ezekiel work and travel together both vertically with God and horizontally with each other. Ezekiel's "Wheel within the wheel," is a biblical prophetic picture of a watch that works and moves together:

"The appearance of the wheels and their workings was like the color of beryl, and all four had the same likeness. The appearance of their workings was, as it were, a wheel in the middle of a wheel. When they moved, they went toward any one of four directions; they did not turn aside when they went. As for their rims, they were so high they were awesome; and their rims were full of eyes, all around the four of them." Ezekiel 3:16-18.

The beauty of an authentic watch is that it does not interfere with established ministry vision/goals, or leadership structures. It does not interfere with personal ministry goals or vision. The wheels of Ezekiel turn together, they do not run over each other, but are responsive to the environment they cover. They move together. Such is the picture of a "Watch." It strengthens all involved. In fact, though prayer may unite a church or ministry, a watch unites prayer. It is a vehicle God is using to unite fragmented ends of the prayer movement together.

THE MINDSET SHIFT:

For many involved in ministry it is an initial mindset "jolt" to think about joining or being a part of a "Watch." There is often a shield of resistance or sense of "threat" that is raised when people ponder joining such an entity. Concerns about what they would be joining, alignment issues etc. are raised. Fear of potential loss of identity, vision, resources, people are real concerns as well as roadblocks.

From our perspective in the call to build up the concept of a "Watch," there is a real need to shift our thinking. It is about our various ministries, and churches joining with others to jointly "tend and keep," the gardens God has given us. There is no loss of identity, visionary purpose, or interference with leadership structure. We simply join the ramparts, continue to build the rampart God has given in prayer and worship, see what God is saying, Habakkuk 2:1, and sound the trumpet when there is alarm, Nehemiah 4:19-20. Healthy relationships can inspire such collaboration without interfering, imposing, or taking from others on the wall. Rather there is a sense of lending a helping hand. Is such a thing possible? Yes. Is it easy? No. Does it require a shift in how we relate and do ministry? Yes.

The wheels of corporate expressions of prayer may arise in private homes, churches, houses of prayer, businesses, college campuses, hospitals, or wherever two or more are gathered on a consistent basis. Watchmen are being raised up in all the cultural spheres with burdens to pray for government, education, businesses, media, entertainment, or families. When these focus specific assignments are connected with committed relentless corporate prayer, the impact is transformational. Watchmen are strong builders. As new assignments are being released, a sign of a watchman is that they will look to build. Where are the streams already flowing and how might joining enhance entities involved? There is a maturing in the body of Christ in these times where the process of building together is not only becoming more necessary but vital to face the challenges.

When we started the "Watch" in our city, we started with a small group committed to the night watch. Praying in our homes on assigned nights, we met once a week to share and pray together. Shortly thereafter, the corporate expression grew with others joining in. Eventually, the neighbors on the street began to complain of the cars and traffic that ensued. In searching for a solution, our church was gracious to open their doors to the meetings. We moved the regional "Watch" sessions there. Soon other churches and a few pastors joined in and continues to this day. Our stance has always been to honor the local church and its leadership. Over the years of praying corporately in this place, the growth in the church housing the "watch" has been amazing. Satellite churches are developing throughout the region and reaching out to the coast. When prayer is honored and becomes a functional part of a church, the church does prosper. Committing to prayer changes things. It might be disconcerting at first, but in the end it will prosper.

In the midst of cultures increasingly resistant to God and His precepts, God is putting a new hunger in people to draw together, to seek His face and His Presence. The foundations for an end-time harvest are being laid before our eyes. Do not despise the days of small beginnings, or be disheartened in a small prayer meeting. God is the great economist. Take your stance as watchmen. Prepare for and declare the harvest that is right around the corner.

APPLICATION:

1. Do you have a clear vision for your life? If not, what can you do to clarify God's call?
2. Is there a specific time when God called you?
3. What were the circumstances?
4. Were there significant confirmations?

Five

THE WATCH: COMMUNITY, COMMITMENT, AND COMMUNICATION

"Trust in the Lord, and do good; dwell in the
land, and feed on His faithfulness. Delight
yourself also in the Lord, and He shall give you
the desires of your heart. Commit your way to
the Lord, trust also in Him, and He shall bring it
to pass. He shall bring forth your righteousness as
the light, and your justice as the noonday."

Psalm 37:3-6

It was 1727. In a quiet little village set in the foothills of eastern Germany, God looked down and watched as the villagers worked to settle their disputes. His plan was about to unfold. Composed of various sects, the village, Herrnhut, was culturally diverse and deeply divided. There were many problems amongst the villagers and the leadership due to the varied cultural backgrounds. These differences fueled subsequent conflicts. The clashes came to a nadir in the Spring of 1727. It was then that the Earl of Herrnhut, Count Nicholas Ludwig von Zinzendorf, began to visit the leadership to see what might be done to foster better relationships. As the villagers committed to prayer and community, the Spirit of the Lord fell and launched a prayer movement that changed the course of Christian history. 24/7 prayer erupted lasting over 150 years, and a massive missions movement released 3,000 missionaries into the nations. Worship exploded into thousands of new songs breaking out from their hearts in Presence inspired and driven meetings. Their powerful hymns are still sung today.

As missionaries were sent out, they knew prayers would be offered for their safety and success. "Once a week, letters from overseas were read to the whole congregation.⁹" Such ongoing connection with missionaries inspired a movement beyond one generation. Its culture reflected the power and impact of relational **community, commitment to prayer, and communication**. What happened in Herrnhut, Germany in 1727 represents a historical model of a "Watch." In fact, the name Herrnhut means the "Lord's Watch."

Today, these same components of community, commitment to prayer, and communication lay the foundations of a corporate watch that can lead to transformation and revival. Many times prayer groups will have their "assignments." However, when they intentionally engage a sense of community in its culture, the elements of the great commandments Jesus' spoke of in Matthew 22:37-40, to love God and to love one another can be transformational. Though simple, these commandments are "great" because they carry "great" weight. "On these commandments are all the law and the prophets," Matthew 22:40.

9 Wemmer, Paul; <u>Count Zinzendorf and the Spirit of the Moravians</u>; Xulon Press 2013; pg 128

COMMUNITY:

The impact of relationships in advancing God's kingdom cannot be under-estimated. Why does Jesus say that upon the great commandments, "hang all the law and the prophets." That is a strong statement. Community is what Jesus expressed in Matthew 16:18 when he described the church as "Ekklesia" for which the "Gates of Hades shall not prevail against." There is power in the community of believers. Count von Zinzendorf is noted as saying, **"There can be no Christianity without community.[10]"**

From the Upper Room in Acts 2:1-4 to today, there is power in corpo-rate prayers of agreement. We have all seen and witnessed powerful answers to our prayers. We are encouraged throughout scriptures to seek intimacy with the Lord individually for the fervent prayers of a righteous man "avails much," James 5:16. Given the times, Hebrews 10:24-25 also exhorts the import of corporate prayer,

> "And let us consider one another in order to stir up love and good works, not forsaking the assembling of ourselves together, as is the manner of some, but exhorting one another, and so much the more as you see the Day approaching."

Relationships value, encourage, and recognize the economy of God being uniquely positioned together for the greater corporate advance. Such rec-ognition unlocks the treasures of heaven instilled in each person. I learned this lesson in a time when the vision God had given me became a "con-suming fire." Vision is vital and can be a mobilizing force in one's life, but without relationships, it cannot be accomplished or fulfilled. My energy,

---

10 http://www.sermonindex.net/modules/articles/index.php?view=article&aid =32366

focus, passion and love was for the vision and His call. It had completely overpowered my heart until one day in a still small voice; I heard the Lord say, "love." It suddenly hit me, I had put vision, and the work of the ministry ahead of the love of the brethren. The reality hit that without love we are nothing. God then took me through a season of re-learning to love and care for others in a new and profound way. Without relationships, gifting becomes blunted or worse yet forced because trust has not yet formed. It is through friendships that this confidence develops. When we trust each other, God can trust us with His Spirit and revelation. In fact, when trouble arises in ministries, it is not because the people involved are not sincere believers, but frequently it is because there is not an understanding built upon a relationship.

Over the years, we have learned that when troubles arise amongst co-laborers in Christ, it is a warning sign that we have gotten ahead of ourselves. It is time to pull back, take a deep breath and evaluate the relationships involved. In fact, a core value in our ministry is the protocol of Matthew 18:15-18 in resolving issues with a brother or sister. We all love to quote the scripture of Matthew 18:19, "Again I say to you that if two of you agree on earth concerning anything that they ask, it will be done for them by My Father in heaven." However, we can quickly forget the import and need to work the required reconciliation in the previous verses first. When valued and prioritized, friendships then can become like a human vessel linked together into which God can pour His Spirit.

Friendship pulls relationships past servant-hood into a mutually respected and trusted place. When Jesus considers us friends, John 15:15, "No longer do I call you servants…but I call you friends," we enter a new realm of trust and intimacy with the Father. This friendship is expressed not only in our relationship with God but how we relate to each other. It is not hard or complicated to get started in developing community. When we first realized the import of community, the Lord spoke to us to simply cultivate what we had been given. Nurturing the sense of community starts first with our families, with our spouses, children, brothers and sisters. Then we can move on to being intentional with other relationships God has placed in our path. God has given us all great equity in the people he has put around us. They are valuable in His sight, and if we can deposit life into them, it is like a bank account that increases in its worth. From one deposit, the investment grows. In spiritual warfare, the enemy is less likely to entice people into misunderstanding, strife, accusation, when relationships are formed and encouraged.

Jesus set the example. It was Jesus who sent the disciples out two by two to minister, Luke 10:1. It was Jesus who chose to pour His time and energy into the twelve disciples and from these twelve, there were the three, and from the three there was the one who stayed at His feet. Those relationships changed the world and course of history.

COMMITMENT TO PRAYER:

In mobilizing ongoing corporate prayer in community, like Herrnhut, there must be an underlying sense of responsibility, of discipline individually and corporately for any sustainability. When this sense of commitment is a core value and understood, it will test our integrity but will draw God's attention. Eventually, His powerful signs will manifest, and His testimony will be glorified. James 4:8 promises, "Draw near to God, and He will draw near to you." Committing to a corporate prayer expression is key to the results we get.

How can you sustain such commitment? The answer is we can't in and of ourselves. The draw is His Presence. It is the desire to be in His Presence and our personal responsibility to the Lord that cultivates such commitment. Personal dedication to seeking the Lord with commitment to participate in a corporate expression is an initial first step. Scriptures promise if we seek Him, we will find Him, Deuteronomy 4:29. A little discipline will lead to desire. Experiencing God's Holy Spirit will then begin to drive us to prayer. Soon, the corporate expression matures and His testimony will start to manifest and momentum builds.

When we first started our journey in mobilizing corporate prayer, we soon learned it was quite a different animal than strategic point focus prayer. "Oh God, oh God, if you don't show up we're toast!" was the cry of our hearts before every meeting. As we pursued the call and pressed forward with the remnant God gave us, we began to realize that He was doing just that. He was showing up! Letting Him have the reign of the meetings, we were frequently surprised at how He led us. Meetings would take a turn and a twist, but in the end, His remarkable testimony would always encourage and spur us on. But it took fighting weariness and the temptation to say it was not that important to go on the evenings set for prayer/worship. It required diligence and determination not to give up.

In Herrnhut, one of the requirements of the leaders was to commit to being at leadership meetings every other week. The villagers in Herrnhut grasped the understanding of commitment not only to prayer but community and life together. This commitment to prayer and community held a vessel together for generations. These commitments are true of other revivals lasting more than a generation. From Bangor, Ireland, to the Knights of St. John Watch, commitment was a key sustaining force. Commitment shaped the character of the community for a sustained revival that lasted generations. There is something about such discipline that is a life source and power to any work. It has the potential to fuel revival beyond a few years into generational strength.

Taking a closer look at "commitment," we are not talking about a "dry," hard, life-draining commitment. Psalm 37:5 speaks to the essence of this resolve, "Commit your way to the Lord, Trust also in Him, and He shall bring it to pass." The Hebrew word for "commit" is "galal." It is the same word used in Genesis 29:3 when Jacob "rolled back" a large stone off the well for sheep to come to drink. It would be the very spot where he would meet Rachel, his future wife, for the first time. It was a meeting that unlocked an amazing love story marinated and tested until its fulfillment was granted seven years later.

Commitment, in light of Jacob's actions, does not come from a "have to" but from a "want to" draw from the well. When we commit to something, some destiny, some call on our lives, the discipline required will lead to desire. As with anything in life, a little bit of training goes a long way. Discipline in what we eat, how we exercise, how we schedule our time, carries fruit and the desire to complete what we are called to do and be. Anyone disciplining himself or herself to go to the workout gym on a regular schedule knows how that draw soon becomes desire. They also know what happens when the training lags, and the work that is required to regain lost ground.

Our youngest son was a very gifted young man both in academics and in athletics. However, the discipline to nurture his abilities started to lag in college. We saw him begin to go down hill. Finally, in utter exasperation, we had to lay down the law about finishing his degree. During that season, he became interested in the military and began to work out with special ops forces. A new life began to erupt in some very dry bones. He disciplined himself in school, and the workouts required. At the earliest possible time, he enlisted in college and after graduation went right into boot camp. Through the discipline and commitment required, he passed through the rigors of special ops training onto the teams, loving every minute of it. He found life in commitment, and it is propelling him into destiny.

Discipline and commitment are often things we sideline or forget in our personal walk with the Lord, ministry, or whatever sphere of influence we may be called. Latching onto it opens a wellspring of life that carries eternal significance, much like Jacob meeting Rachel at the well. Roll back the complacency or the "I'll wait for the unction of the Holy Spirit to do it." See what happens when we put our determined and committed foot in the Jordan and watch the waters part.

When people commit not only to pray but to a community, the stone is rolled back, and a wellspring of life comes forth. The springs of living water can open for the sheep to come and drink. When they come to this well, life changes, destiny comes into place, and purpose becomes fulfilled. Commitment breeds longevity, life, and promises fulfilled.

COMMUNICATION:

Communication is a vital component to any community. Without it there is no possibility or means to relate. How we interact and communicate is distinctive of the cultures in which we participate and live in. Moravian's committed to reading communications weekly from their missionaries.[11] Such action continued to propel the purposes of God in their meetings in spite of being in different localities across the nations.

A distinctive of a watchman is that they will make efforts to communicate and intentionally connect with other watchmen. Ezekiel 3:17 states, "Son of man, I have made you a watchman for the house of Israel, therefore hear a word from My mouth, and give them warning from Me." Watchmen are uniquely called to herald the alarm for the urgent issues of the hour. However, the connection, community, and commitment to pray must be in place for it to be effective. If we blow the trumpet but are not connected… what good is it? Nehemiah 4:19-20 says it well, "The work is great and extensive, and we are separated from one another on the wall. Wherever

---

11 Wemmer, pg 128

you hear the sound of the trumpet, rally to us there. Our God will fight for us." To be effective, communication is required. Knowing what and how to respond requires participation, interaction, and frequently wisdom.

Modern day technology allows alerts, news, testimonies to travel the globe in seconds. Such communication, which was not in place ten years ago, has now made it possible for information and alerts to be sent quickly and efficiently. It is possible now to build community not only in our physical environments but also now on a global level. Even in impoverished nations cell phone use makes such communication possible. When relationships develop across international lines, suddenly the news takes on whole new meaning. Our prayers go to a new depth knowing people in the nations and regions.

One such example of mobilized prayer across nations happened in October 2015. Hurricane Patricia formed over the Pacific Ocean. It rallied its power into the largest recorded hurricane in the Western Hemisphere,[12] and the second largest storm recorded worldwide.[13] Watchmen were alerted along the western coast of America from Alaska to Southern California. When the hurricane struck the coast of Mexico, it split in two and became a tropical storm with very little damage. We later found out others in Mexico were also praying in corporate agreement. Corporate cooperative prayer averted one of the largest storms in history.

BALANCING ACT:

As we have seen, the role of community, commitment to prayer/worship are very real characteristics of a "watch" and cannot be underestimated. It is also important to balance them. We can often have community or

---

12 http://www.telegraph.co.uk/news/worldnews/centralamericaandthecaribbean/mexico/11949942/Hurricane-Patricia-strongest-storm-on-record-as-it-barrels-toward-Mexico.html

13 https://en.wikipedia.org/wiki/Hurricane_Patricia

commitment to prayer in our various ministry assignments, but frequently do not see both or they are out of balance. It has been a travesty to see people come out of the prayer room or church and run into fights and differences outside the door. Or people engaged in their community, doing great works in their spiritual environments, but not going back to the "Well" from which our strength comes. It is easy to slip and "lop-side" one and not the other getting us quickly out of balance.

When the value of relationships with others balances with our personal walk with the Lord, community life begins to be experienced. Such community cultivates order through the recognition only relationship promotes. The early church understood these values, and as a result, the church exploded onto the face of the earth. Acts 2:46-47 relays the fact that the early church not only worshipped in the temple, but in smaller group settings in their homes.

"So continuing daily **with one accord in the temple, and breaking bread from house to house,** they ate their food with gladness and simplicity of heart, praising God and having favor with all the people. And the Lord added to the church daily those who were being saved." Acts 2:46-47

Worship, prayer in joyful, care inspiring community are keys for a great and lasting revival that last beyond a few short years. These keys are eternal truths, easily applied to any church or culture. The result could lead the church into a great end-time harvest and revival that will have no end.

These concepts are not new, but with renewed intentionality carry significant spiritual weight. The understanding of caring community life founded on intentional seeking the Lord carried the message of the Gospel across the nations with a fiery force. During the lifetime of the

Apostles, Christianity had spread across the Hellenistic world and beyond the Roman Empire. By the end of the first century, Christianity was a recognized religion.

With times intensifying, a great "Awakening" is knocking at the door of the church. Those who hear it are now moving to "Rise and build," to reach out to their communities, seek new ways to collaborate, and cultivate community. Ancient walls of division are crashing to the ground as people, joined in community, commitment to prayer, and communication, move forward compelled by God to worship, pray, and build.

APPLICATION:

1. Take time to evaluate your family life. What can you do to cultivate community within your family?
2. What relationships in your work/ministry sphere do you want to be intentional in developing?
3. How would evaluate the balance between work and community in your ministry/work environment? Are they in the balance or out of balance? If out of balance, what can you do about it?

Six

STIR AND SPUR LIFE!

"And let us consider one another in order to
stir up love and good works, not forsaking the
assembling of ourselves together, as is the manner
of some but exhorting one another, and so much
more as you see the Day approaching."

Hebrews 10:24-25

In discussion with a group of ministry leaders, we were talking about the
need for leaders to have support and community. As the discussion got
rather heated over the concern, one of the pastor's threw up his hands and
cried, "I don't have a community!" It caused us all to take a deep breath as
he was a much loved and respected pastor. It was like a shock wave hit the
room and we all were at a loss for words as the raw truth hit the table. But,
as the revelation struck our hearts, it broke open a reality and strategy that
began to break the ice.

A few months later, we held a "House HOP" three nights in a row, for
various ministry groups in our church. What we called a "House HOP"
(House of Prayer) was simply a gathering for fun, food, and fellowship
followed by prayer and worship in community. On the first night, people

came in happy but somewhat curious about this "new thing." As we set out the food and began the fellowship, I asked one of the older women, known for her prayer life, to say a prayer over the group. In a rather trepidatious manner, she stepped forward. But suddenly as she stood up tall, words came out of her that hit the room like a machine gun from heaven. Everyone in the room lit up. Any ounce of complacency was gone as smiles; laughter filled the atmosphere. Pastors picked up guitars and started singing, people began to pray for one another, and the ministry of Jesus came forth through the hearts and attitudes of those attending. At one point, I looked around the room to see pastors, laity, children, young and old praying for one another, encouraging, laughing together as the Spirit of the Lord spoke quietly to my heart saying, "this is unity."

Something unique happened during those three days. The culture of the church shifted. Relationships became warmer and more friendly. Community and the sense of the love of the Lord flowing amongst His people broke through. Genuine care and concern for those around us escalated. The spiritual climate changed. What was it? Community. Barriers of professionalism, gender, age, culture came crashing to the floor. Everyone could feel the genuine love of the Lord.

What inspires such a culture to survive and prosper? It is worth taking a look at keys that cultivate healthy environments among believers and what is emerging from them.

THE POWER OF BLESSING: SPEAK LIFE!

A joyful atmosphere does much to dispel the power of the enemy over any corporate gathering. Deuteronomy 30:19 relays, "I call heaven and earth as witnesses today against you, that I have set before you life and death, blessing and cursing; therefore choose life, that both you and your descendants may live." We learned early on in corporate prayer ministry to start sessions with participants blessing each other. We discovered that sessions starting with speaking blessing were by far easier to engage with than those starting off "stone cold." Much was dispelled by this simple act. The difficulties of the day melted away under a positive environment, and people were much more ready to engage in worship/prayer.

There is much in the Bible about the impact of the tongue. Proverbs 18:21 states, "Death and life are in the power of the tongue." Furthermore, Jesus said and walked out His words, "But I say to you, love your enemies, bless those who curse you, and pray for those who spitefully use you and persecute you," Matthew 5:44. Why? By purposefully blessing those who curse you, it is like a knife that frees you from the grip of a "tare," something that holds you back, and places you under the blessing of the Lord. It also releases those who are the source of the potential offense under the hand of the Lord. He knows much more about how to deal with the issues than we do.

A useful tool to encourage walking in the power of the blessing is to commit to a personal or corporate Isaiah 58:9 fast. Isaiah 58:9 states, "If you take away the yoke from your midst. The pointing of the finger and speaking wickedness." Take a 40 day fast and refuse to speak or think negatively towards every situation or person you come in contact with. During the fast, determine to speak a blessing to those around you and view your circumstances in God's redemptive light. Such a fast is helpful for "watchman seers" with the gift of discernment. Stopping the pointing of the finger reduces tendency towards negativity and "Woe is me," attitudes that can easily rise. Seeking the blessing in all circumstances helps us see the bigger liberating plan of God. Isaiah 58:12 goes on to promise, "Those from among you shall build the old waste places; you shall raise up the foundations of many generations, and you shall be called the Repairer of the Breach, the Restorer of Streets to Dwell in." It is a powerful result of walking in the blessing.

In a ministry in which we are heavily involved, the slogan amongst the youth and young adults is, "We love you no matter what!" Such a motto prevents offense from settling in. In sticky situations, just saying those words puts a smile on people's faces and shields against offense with effective results. In fact, when you get around the atmosphere of such positivity and grace, the power of any curse cannot prevail. It is completely shoved out of the conversation and the room. The power of blessing is an actual magnet that draws the Lord's Presence and opens the door for the Lord to move. The message from Proverbs 10:22, "The blessing of the Lord makes one rich, and He adds no sorrow to it," actually works! It is the message of the gospel in a nutshell! And there is no condemnation in it.

MINISTRY OF RECOGNITION:

When building a sense of community, consideration for one another is fostered when people are honorably acknowledged for who they are, and the strength they bring to the body of Christ. A foundational moment for the birth of the New Testament church was through the ministry of recognition. Jesus pulled the disciples 30 miles out of the way to Caesarea Philippi, a spiritually dark place. He set them down in front of a cave known for its demonic activity, to teach them. In front of these "gates of hell," He asks His disciples, "Who do you say that I am?" Matthew 16:15. Some of the disciples hemmed and hawed, but it was Peter who blurted, "You are the Christ." There in front of the gates of hell, heaven opened and its storehouse released. Peter recognized Jesus for who He was. It was here Jesus declared, "On this rock, I will build My church (the Ekklesia), and the gates of Hades shall not prevail against it," Matthew 16:18. Not only that, Jesus promises Peter,

"I will give you the keys of the kingdom of heaven, and whatever you bind on earth will be bound in heaven, and whatever you loose on earth will be loosed in heaven," Matthew 16:19. Through recognition, the will of heaven and its resources were made manifest on earth. From this point on, Jesus' ministry changed from ministering to the people to a focus on Jerusalem. He was released into His destiny and purpose for life on earth. Ekklesia is an important concept that Pastor Greg Simas will address at the end of the book.

The ministry of recognition is a powerful tool in advancing the Kingdom and the growth of a church or ministry. Does it mean we have to sit around a "Rah, rah" table with endless compliments? No! But it does mean we take the time to acknowledge, and value other people and their gifts, and get beyond superficial conversation. It is amazing to watch enemy assignments fall away once people are recognized for who they are. Once recognition of a person's strengths and giftings are verbalized, the resources that person brings to the table are more readily understood, and utilized. Heaven's supply lines are released and all are empowered. I am convinced that this single ministry in its simplicity is highly underutilized, keeping much of the church disempowered. In environments where it is utilized, many are released into their God-given assignments with clarity and purpose. Jealousy, and envy that may have been significant undercurrents holding back the promises of God are suddenly halted. Value, honor, integrity, and strategy are then released for the advance of the kingdom.

KEEP THE HOUSE CLEAN:

The enemy hates corporate prayer because of its power. In the corporate prayer environment, the verses out of Matthew 18:19-20 are often quoted with great enthusiasm and assurance of God's Word working together in our prayers,

> "Again I say to you that if two of you agree on earth concerning anything that they ask, it will be done for them by My Father in heaven, for where two of three are gathered together in My name, I am there in the midst of them." Matthew 18:19-20.

However, what is not often mentioned is the protocol described in the previous verses. These Scriptures deal with our offenses. In other words, our prayers of agreement are powerful when we have first reconciled with our brothers. Matthew 18:10-18 relay the protocol to best deal with offenses that rise amongst brethren:

- Go to the person individually to sort out the issues; if he hears you, you will have gained a friend.
- If that doesn't work, take with you one or two others
- And if that doesn't work, take it to the church /ministry involved
- If he refuses to hear, then let him be to you like a heathen.

These Scriptures outline wise protocol. We believe strongly in this order and encourage all to follow it. Unfortunately, the protocol is often reversed, where public opinion is spewed forth before the person involved has a chance to clarify or give the explanation. Using this protocol out of step can frequently put God's divine plan in jeopardy. Too often, I have heard the public announcement of a misstep by someone before anyone has spoken to the offender. The enemy hates corporate prayer and will use any venue, vessel, to disrupt it. Handling offenses in the body of Christ are vital to keeping the community prayer environment safe, vibrant and healthy.

WALK IN INTEGRITY:

"As for me, You uphold me in my integrity, and set me before Your face forever," Psalm 41:12. Integrity is fashioned in the secret place. God is more concerned about who we are than what we do. On a regular basis, the "who we are" tests will often come before the "what we do" opportunities.

When called to mobilize prayer in community, do not be alarmed at the retribution, misunderstanding, or backlash that occurs. The enemy hates corporate prayer because it is a distinct blockade and attack against his designs on a person or community. In the midst of the attack, watch your tongue! We have often been exhorted by David's plea in Psalm 39:1-3:

"I said, 'I will guard my ways, lest I sin with my tongue; I will restrain my mouth with a muzzle, While the wicked are before me.'
I was mute with silence, I held my peace even from good, and my sorrow was stirred up. My heart was hot within me."

Walk determinedly to bless those who curse you. Be willing to serve others, even in the secret place where there is no outward reward. Such action puts you under the protection of the Lord. Psalm 15:1-5 speaks of the import of integrity.

"Lord, who may abide in Your tabernacle? Who may dwell in Your holy hill?
He who walks uprightly, And works righteousness, And speaks the truth in his heart; He who does not backbite with his tongue, Nor does evil to his neighbor, Nor does he take up a reproach

against his friend; In whose eyes a vile person is despised, But he honors those who fear the Lord; He who swears to his own hurt and does not change; He who does not put out his money at usury, Nor does he take a bribe against the innocent. He who does these things shall never be moved."

It is His promise, if we walk in integrity, we shall never be moved, and He will uphold us in His presence forever.

FAMILY: FROM NEXT GENERATION TO NEW GENERATION:

There is a phenomenon growing out of the millennial generation today. A supernatural turning of hearts is happening between generations. Youth and young adults from war-torn families are coming out of the streets hungry for the real thing. Out of the moral and spiritual struggles today, the reality of Malachi 4:6 is taking place, "And he will turn the hearts of the fathers to the children and the children to the fathers." The decades of "free speech," individualism of the '60's and 70's sowed seeds of rebellion leading to separation and isolation of the generations in the ensuing years. Subsequently, there has been an emergence and dependence on street drugs and defilement of family values. This resistance has resulted in a multi-generational increase of "fatherlessness." In the midst of this, however, a remarkable turn is taking place. Young adults, having gone to the depths of despair in lifestyles enshrouded in drugs, sex, rebellion, are coming to the end of themselves. Seeking the reality of the true and living God, they are emerging, hungry for the context of "real" family.

God is watching over His word of Malachi 4:6, "And he will turn the hearts of the fathers to the children and the children to the fathers." The wisdom of the older generation is merging with the vigor of the younger generation. The years of reconciliation in the prayer movement is beginning to pay off. Vision not yet accomplished in the older generation, is being established through this convergence. Where this merging is occuring, Psalm 71:18-20, is happening:

"Now also when I am old and grayheaded, O God, do not forsake me, until I declare Your strength to this generation, Your power to everyone who is to coe. Also Your reighteousness, O God, is very high, You who have done great things; O God, who is like You? You, who have shown me great and severe troubles shall revive me again!"

If this convergence around you is not happening, pray for it! A respect amongst the generations is rising and much is being accomplished through the relationships forming. The younger generation gains the advantage of learning from the older generation who have walked through their valleys giving them wisdom they would not have otherwise. The older generation is gaining the advantage of being "revived" and renewed through the vigor and zeal of the youth.

Within a community, the sense of family is the foundation upon which all things grow. The understanding of family is essential as it is God's first governmental form on earth. In healthy families, each person has a role. The member's varied strengths and weaknesses are recognized and used to sharpen one another. Even though the differences may cause friction, in healthy families, there is enough relational strength to bridge and build in spite of differences. Such rapport in a family fosters respect. There is respect for one another, and enough relationship not only to tolerate but appreciate the personalities involved. No one is perfect, but love is the balm that keeps the gears going.

In its healthiest form, a community will be actively involved in mentoring and discipleship. Jesus did not say in His great commission to go "save," but to go make "disciples" of all nations, Matthew 28:19. As the inter-generational barriers are breaking, mentoring and discipleship are moving into important and vital forces in the body of Christ.

One of the most encouraging ministries we are involved in is "Encounter" nights with youth and young adults. In the atmosphere of shared home-cooked potluck meals, fellowship, worship prayer, the young adults are hungry for mentorship, relationship. Many come from very stressful family environments, from unbelieving backgrounds to drug, gang, and alternative lifestyles. Encounter nights balance community with committed prayer, and it has never failed for God to show up. People have been baptized in the pool, received deliverance, and encountered the reality of Christ in their lives. In the midst, we see an emergence of a "new" generation leadership and it is fostering life and health to all involved.

FROM ELIJAH TO ELISHA:

A shift is already happening. God's Spirit is pouring out new revelation. Joel 2:28 prophecies, "And it shall come to pass afterward that I will pour out My Spirit on all flesh; your sons and your daughters shall prophesy, and your old men shall see visions." A vital restoration of prophetic ministry to the church is underway. Jesus said, "Indeed, Elijah is coming first and will restore all things," Matthew 17:11. The spirit of Elijah is already at work. As God pours out His Spirit for an end-time harvest, the prophetic ministry is being restored and raised up through local church expressions, Christian ministries, communities to the nations. Prophetic seers, the watchmen, are rising across the nations. Forerunners with prophetic mantles have already been sent to restore such ministry to the church. Through their work, doors are beginning to open for more revelation and understanding of this important ministry to be an active part of church culture. Paul exhorts the New Testament church,

"Pursue love, and desire spiritual gifts, but especially that you may prophesy. For he who speaks in a tongue does not speak to men but to God, for no one understands him; however, in the spirit he speaks mysteries. But he who prophesies speaks edification and exhortation and comfort to men." 1 Corinthians 14:1-4

It is vital for any church or ministry moving forward to understand and utilize the prophetic gift. The younger generation is moving into prophetic revelation because God is moving in them. The danger now lies in not mentoring or encouraging healthy prophetic atmospheres that work with present leadership structures in the church. A new generation is now emerging to bring the refreshing of Elisha to the body of Christ. Much like the relationship between Elijah and Elisha, generation to generation, in its healthiest form, prophetic ministry will be cultivated and have an active mentorship and accountability in place. The double portion generation of Elisha is coming forward. It is here! It behooves the body of Christ and the church to listen, hear, receive it, and work with it.

RUN THE RACE WITH ENDURANCE, AND HIS JOY BE OUR STRENGTH!

Many forging the battleground to mobilize and establish community corporate prayer have had to face headwinds of resistance from outside and from within. From complacency to outright opposition, the headwinds have been strong. In an event-driven culture where numbers mean everything, those called to the prayer room have had the humble

STIR AND SPUR LIFE!

privilege of seeing the few show on a consistent basis and yet forge ahead. In such circumstances, we have learned unceasing regular corporate prayer is not about numbers but about apprehending the heart of God and agreement.

The Moravians understood the concept of the need to endure the opposition and persecution in order to "run the race" to establish prayer in their home and missions efforts. Under accusations from neighboring nobles, Count von Zinzendorf was exiled for ten years from his beloved Germany. He used the opportunity to spread the gospel and earned the title of the "Pilgrim Count" during that time.[14] Many Moravians died on the mission field having been faithful to their call. In the face of opposition, a key to spiritual success was their stance, and the joy of the Lord was their strength. They did not give in to the oppression, depression, and discouragement the enemy likes to impose. Cathryn Booth, co-founder of the Salvation Army, poignantly describes what often happens to those burning in zeal for the Lord,

> "True saints are might, and their heat will make more impression on the hearts of sinners and stir more opposition from hell than all the intellect and learning of a whole generation of lukewarm professors. True saints ensure opposition from the Pharisees, the casual, weekend religious professors who are not true possessors.[15]"

In such a battle, joy is a remarkable instrument of God's strength. The Moravians understood, lived and modeled joy. In his words, Count von

---

14 https://en.wikipedia.org/wiki/Nicolaus_Zinzendorf
15 Wemmer, pg. 120

Zinzendorf reflected such an impressive attitude. On a ride through the woods with host and co-laborers, Count von Zinzendorf records an encounter with religious questioning. His calm sense of humor is reflected in this encounter.,

> "In the course of conversation, put a number of indifferent and idle questions on religious subjects. My inability to answer him gratified rather than chagrined me, and was, I thought, altogether an advantage on my side.[16]"

May we too be exhorted by Hebrews 12:1-2 and keep joy a central focus of our call as Watchmen, "Let us run with endurance the race that is set before us, looking unto Jesus the author and finisher of our faith, who for the joy that was set before Him, endured the cross, despising the shame, and has sat down at the right hand of the throne of God."

NEW SONG RISING:
When community, committed prayer, and communication interweave, a culture of revival emerges, and a transformational process begins. In such settings, worship cannot be held in restraint and "familiar" territory. The heart breaks open and new songs rise. In biblical history, reforms and revivals were marked by the release of music and the "new song." The Psalms are filled with new songs, many written by David in the transition and reformation in David's time. Hezekiah, Josiah's reforms were all marked by re-establishment of temple worship (2 Chronicles 29:20; 2 Kings 23).

---

16 Count Nicholas von Zinzendorf, William Reichel, Martin Mack, <u>Memorials of the Moravian Church</u>, J.P. Lippincott & Co., Philadelphia, 1870, pg 51

Music and song is a conduit in which God communicates His message to earth. Psalm 40:2-3 declares how a new song heralds the spiritual shift, "He also brought me up out of a horrible pit, out of the miry clay, and set my feet upon a rock, and established my steps. He has put a new song in my mouth-Praise to our God; many will see it and fear, and will trust in the Lord."

The influence of music from the Moravians reached the church of England, and into the missions movement and to the ends of the earth. Their music and mission through community, committed prayer, and communication influenced figures such as William Carey, and John and Charles Wesley. Charles Wesley had more than 6,000 hymns published after his conversion through the works and witness of one of the early Moravian missionaries, Peter Boehler.[17] In fact, today, as watchmen take their place in their communities, it would be well to listen for the new songs of worship. Such praise is a sign that God has heard. His Spirit is moving. Transforming revival is emerging, and the new song is rising.

> Oh for a thousand tongues to sing
> My dear Redeemer's praise
> The glories of my God and King
> The triumphs of His grace.
> He breaks the power of canceled sin,
> He sets the prisoner free;
> His blood can make the foulest clean,
> His blood availed for me.[18]

---

17 http://www.evanwiggs.com/revival/history/moravian.html
18 http://www.evanwiggs.com/revival/history/moravian.html

(song written by Charles Wesley shortly after his conversion in 1738 through Moravian missionary Peter Boehler)

APPLICATION:

1. What area in your life and spiritual walk would you like encouragement or mentoring?
2. Who or what in your life has been been a particular obstacle difficult to defeat? Are you free from any curses the person or incident placed on you? What could you do to come under the canopy of blessing?
3. Are there people in your life that could encourage your development? If so, how might you cultivate a relationship with them to strengthen your walk?

Seven

RELENTLESS...

"I have set watchmen on your walls, O Jerusalem; they shall never hold their peace day or night. You who make mention of the Lord, do not keep silent, and give Him no rest till He establishes and till He makes Jerusalem a praise in the earth."

Isaiah 62:6-7

It was a Monday evening. I was on the road to the weekly evening "Watch" for our city and county. I was exhausted. So much so, it felt like I was functioning on my last cell and nerve. Mechanically, opening the doors to the prayer room, I somehow got the basic set up going. My husband, Fred, came in shortly after that. I quietly told him that I really could not help lead that night. In my state of exhaustion, I could not for the life of me get myself into the state of prayer and worship, let alone help anyone else. In his kind manner, he agreed. I went to the furthest corner of the room, and put my back against the wall, and slid down into a sitting position. I hemmed myself in the corner of the room, shut my eyes, and just totally concentrated on taking another breath, as my mind, will and emotions completely shut down.

People came into the room, and pretty soon the worship started. Opening my eyes, I saw people engage in fervent, joyous worship. Smiles were on their faces and joy filled the room. I just simply agreed with them but remained in shutdown mode. However, as the worship built momentum, something suddenly shifted. My heart turned to Him, not to my problems, weariness, and exhaustion. Suddenly, as my spirit began to agree with the worship, my mind will, and emotions came under the Holy Spirit's influence. Bit, by bit, the weariness dropped off as new life began to course through my body. As I submitted to the worship, the Holy Spirit in resurrection power flooded my entire being. Before long, I was on two feet, feeling better than if I had eight hours of sleep. Prayers came forth with wisdom and revelation and the night became fully electrified in the Presence of the Lord.

That day, I experienced, in a personal way, the resurrection power of the Holy Spirit, and the value of commitment to overcome the obstacles that were keeping me from His Presence. "Relentless," became a reality for me that night. If I had not committed to staying and had turned around to go back home, I would never have had the encounter. What God did in a few short moments of supernatural, surrendered worship, was more than what would have taken perhaps several days to overcome in the natural.

As tribulation and judgments increase, the call for these "relentless" ones is rising. What is the character of men and women that inspire them to "not keep silent" day or night even in the face of opposition? What is it that gives them such staying power particularly in prayer and in days of adversity? What drives them to their knees relentlessly seeking the Lord of Hosts? Discovery of the drivers for such ceaseless desire opens the pathway to the throne room of heaven as Revelation 4:1 beckons, "After these things I looked, and behold, a door standing open in heaven. And the first voice which I heard was like a trumpet speaking with me saying, 'Come up here, and I will show you things which must come after this.'"

THE CALL TO THE RELENTLESS:

The battleground for watchmen is great. The enemy knows if he can knock us out of position, out of our call to "tend and keep" the garden he has given us, he has won the battle and can take the territory. The first garden God gives us to watch over is our identity...who God created us to be. Part of our identity is our gifts and callings. They were formed in our "mother's womb before we were born," Psalm 139:13. As such, they are vital for us to "Watch over."

Romans 11:29 makes it clear, "The gifts and calling of God are irrevocable." There is a call of God that is part of our natural being or more specifically our spiritual identity. In other words, the calling of God in our lives is without repentance. Psalm 139 goes on to relay this call:

"For You formed my *inward parts*; You covered me in my mother's womb. I will praise You, for I am fearfully and wonderfully made; Marvelous are Your works, and that my soul knows very well. My frame was not hidden from You, when I was made in secret, and skillfully wrought in the lowest parts of the earth. Your eyes saw my substance, being yet unformed. And in Your book they all were written, the days fashioned for me when as yet there were none of them. How precious also are Your thoughts to me, O God! How great is the sum of them!" Psalm 139:13-17

What an awesome thought that God formed our *inward parts*! Think about it! God makes no mistakes. He created our inner workings, not just our body, but our mind, will, and emotions, the "inner drive," the things that make us tick. The word parts, or in Hebrew *kilya*, means not just physical organs, but also our mind, our seat of emotions…how we think, respond. Like an engine that makes a car move, He has formed our inward parts. Our inward parts drive our lives. The more "tuned" an engine is, the better it drives and the more likely it will get us to the place we are to go. The place we are to go is in His plans. Jeremiah 29:11 promises God has a plan for us, "to prosper us and not to harm us, to give us a hope and a future," Jeremiah 29:11. Within that plan is the working out of the irrevocable gifts and call of God. Though our bodies may waste away, the inner parts, our engine, are what sustain us through thick and thin. Our gifts and calling are spiritual DNA God created within us as watchmen that will sustain us through thick and thin.

Often, we think of the enemy legally accessing our lives through our weaknesses, our failures. That is true; he will use any means to keep us from understanding the goodness of God and working out God's full measure in our lives. It is important to humble ourselves, as Psalm 139:24 goes on to say, "And see if there is any wicked way in me and lead me in the way everlasting." But also seek the revelation of God.

THE TESTING OF OUR STRENGTHS:

Even more strategically, the enemy will target our strengths. In fact, the stronger the call on your life, the more powerful the attacks may be. Repeated accusations, failures, often may point to an actual strength, a destiny of God, within us. The more attacked we are in a particular area, the more likely the enemy is targeting something he does not want us to see, acknowledge, or walk in. God, on the other hand, desires to strengthen us, to be "strong and do great exploits," Daniel 11:32. He wants us to learn to wield the sword (His Word), with accuracy and strength. Chewing on accusations, continuing to condemn ourselves in our failures, is exactly what the enemy wants us to do. In that way, he can blind us to our true identity. Our failures can be mighty fields for the harvest of wisdom. Trials are the spiritual workout gyms that God uses to build and condition our spiritual muscle. How we handle and process the difficulties makes all the difference as to the outcome.

One time, in particular, I went through a significant testing and a "dryness" where His Presence seemed far away no matter what I did. Unjust accusations had risen towards the very calling God had given me without any understanding or searching out of the history or the circumstances. As I sought the Lord over the situation, my worship, prayer, quiet time in the Word seemed dry as the desert. I could not figure out what was the blockage. I was frustrated with the unjustified accusations and could not shake them. Seeking discernment, I sought counsel from a friend about the onslaught. She simply smiled at me and said, "Congratulations, this is your graduation day!" I looked at her incredulously and could not even think of a word to respond.

I knew God was testing my character, but the assignment did not break. I rehearsed Matthew 5:11-12 repeatedly in my quiet time,

"Blessed are you when they revile and persecute you, and say all kinds of evil against you falsely for My sake. Rejoice and be exceedingly glad, for great is your reward in heaven, for so they persecuted the prophets who were before you," Matthew 5:11-12.

I obediently followed the command of Matthew 5:44, "But I say to you, love your enemies, bless those who curse you, do good to those who hate you, and pray for those who spitefully use you and persecute you." Seeking the Lord in prayer gave me some hope, but yet the condemnation did not break. Finally, one morning I woke up on my usual 4th watch prayer time.

The Lord prompted me to move into worship before I did anything else. I did not ask Him anything or dive into His Word. I did not turn on worship music but with arms outstretched, completely surrendered to Him. In the midst of the worship, I heard Him say, "They are my children too." I knew what the Lord was saying. Suddenly, light fell on a dark area of my heart. The entire assignment of accusation broke. I began to weep for the individuals involved. I cried out to God to forgive me for holding offense. Suddenly, my heart opened with love for them, and I began to pray for them out of love, not out of obligation and obedience to His Word, but out of love.

God spoke that beautiful morning. I heard what He said to me. The season of searching, seeking Him in worship and the Word culminated in an encounter with His love. Worship, studying His Word, diligently seeking Him through the test were assignments to serve Him. But the morning of the breakthrough into experiencing His love, was the morning when I shifted from being a servant to being His friend. I understood John 15:15 like never before, "No longer do I call you servants, for a servant, does not know what his master is doing; but I have called you friends, for all things that I heard from My Father I have made known to you." That morning, the Lord showed me to stand in my calling. The test taught me to "tend and keep" the gift and calling within me. The enemy had to flee. God revealed to me what was in His heart. My engine emerged, totally recharged and ignited by His love. It was a supernatural engine make-over, and I was ready to relentlessly, more than ever, pursue him.

Therefore, count it all joy and be strong and of good courage, withstand the darts of the enemy and trust in Him. God uses these tests to strengthen us.

THE STRENGTH TO STAND:

Aligning ourselves with our spiritual identity, using our gifts and calling, will always test our character. God is more concerned about who we are than what we do. As Watchmen, there is a high call to "Stand." Again, a central verse for Watchmen is Habakkuk 2:1 in which it calls us to "Stand" our watch. In Ephesians 6, the command to "stand" is mentioned three times in the command to put on the full armor of God. "And having done all, to stand," Ephesians 6:13, is a high call and challenge.

In fact, the greater the calling, the greater the tests. After many significant trials, Abraham was 100 when he received the promise of his calling. Moses was 80 when he led the children of Israel through the desert. Job had lost everything before he gained anything. All were diligent "Watchmen" over the calling God had for them. But because of the calling, the tests were not easy, and it took time to generate the character. As we learn to rely on God through the tests, God develops our character and stamina for the greater work ahead.

Zechariah 4:10 challenges, "Who has despised the day of small things?" God is faithful, and sometimes it is the most insignificant, unseen things we do that carry the weight of heaven. Mary and Joseph understood this concept. Mary carried the Savior of the world in her womb, and yet she was not offended to give birth in a stable. Anyone who has walked in a stable knows how it smells and how dirty it is. Is this the place that would be regarded by men as a miracle or where the anticipated Messiah would be born? Perhaps God used the least and lowly place to test the hearts of men.

As we commit to stand "Watch," using the various gifts and callings He has given us, God trusts us. As we draw near to God, He draws near to us. Commitment is a key to standing in a relentless pursuit of God. The "Samar" stance, the "Keeping" part, of the Watchman, requires commitment lest we be like chaff in the wind tossed to and fro by the headwinds of enemy schemes. Every success and victory in the Bible required commitment to accomplish. Ephesians 4 speaks of the unity in the body of Christ brought through sound equipping in who we are called to be and do. Ephesians 4:14 exhorts,

> "That we should no longer be children, tossed to and fro and carried about with every wind of doctrine, by the trickery of men, in the cunning craftiness of deceitful plotting, but, speaking the truth in love, may grow up in all things into Him who is the head-Christ."

In today's world, commitment is a really hard concept to truly grasp. In an age of convenience in prosperity, on the one hand; or entitlement recycling poverty on the other, there is a resistance to taking a stand and committing. We can succumb to the "I'll just wait until the Holy Spirit tells me." Yes, it is important to be always listening to the Lord. But, it is also important once He has spoken to be obedient to follow. When we commit, God entrusts us with watching over His covenant and His plan:

> "As for you, you shall *keep* (samar) My covenant, you and your descendants after you throughout their generations. This is My covenant which you shall keep, between Me and you and your descendants after you." Genesis 17:9

We have heard stories of pastors who have responded to the call of God to turn their churches back to the functional dynamic of a "House of Prayer," only to find a few people show up and their numbers decline. They have forged the battle and have been willing to commit and "pray the price" only to witness the power of God to increase.

God trained us by holding corporate "watch" meetings in our local community for years. In the process, we learned the ins and outs of what it takes to sustain such an entity. It seemed like a small thing as we were just a small group in a humble and not very regarded community. When we went to large meetings with successful Houses of Prayer, we were often intimidated and humbled with the reality that our house was a prayer room with a small consistent group of people who gathered to simply worship, pray, get into His Presence and hear what He was saying. However, it was here we learned to be attentive to His voice, what it means to stand with integrity, to be committed in the face of difficult headwinds. We learned the value of discipline, and to honor and value one another through thick and thin. But most of all, we learned to love Him no matter what the circumstances. God's call for the body of Christ is to "take up the whole armor of God, that you may be able to withstand in the evil day, and having done all to stand," Ephesians 6:13, in the face of the onslaught. In response, He does the rest. He is faithful to complete the good work He has started in us.

APPLICATION:

1. What are your gifts and calling_____?
2. Are you using them? If not, why?
3. What are your strengths and weaknesses? How has God used both?

Eight

RISE AND BUILD: CALL TO THE WALL

"You also, as living stones, are being built up a
spiritual house, a holy priesthood, to offer up
spiritual sacrifices acceptable to God through
Jesus Christ."

1 Peter 2:5

What role does a watchman play in the context of the present day church? If we are all called to "watch," given God's purpose for creating man, what is distinctive about a "Watchman?" Given the current culture of violence, lawlessness, terrorism erupting nearly everywhere you look, one might ask how "Tending and keeping," the garden God gave us works today.

Tending and keeping requires active engagement with the Lord. Ezekiel was called to be a watchman for Israel, Ezekiel 3:17. The Lord spoke to him saying, "You shall hear a word from My mouth and warn them for Me," Ezekiel 33:7. These words relay a watchman's intimate relationship with the Lord. John Eckhardt notes, "Without a revelation of the *"Samar"* ("keep") aspect of the prophetic ministry, a local church will suffer from many attacks that can be averted.[19]"

The very nature of a watchman in Habbakuk 2:1, "I will stand my watch and set myself on the rampart and watch to see what He will say to me," carries the connotation and call of one who looks ahead, a 'forerunner.' This verse implies a watchfulness and readiness for action, for something yet to come. Such a calling is described in Hebrews 6:20,

> "This hope we have as an anchor of the soul, both sure and steadfast, and which enters the Presence behind the veil, where the *forerunner* has entered for us, even Jesus, having become High Priest forever according to the order of Melchizedek."

This scripture describes those called as forerunners, those who are to go ahead, to pioneer into new territory. They scout out situations, make observations, and prepare a place for the "troops to land." Called by God, they have pressed beyond the veil of common ordinary life, comfort zones, and familiar environments to forge ahead into new territory. As such, not only are watchmen fore-runners, but they are ready builders. Though not often understood in their calling, given time, these pioneers look back to see others begin to take the trail they have forged. In God's time, faces, and conversations suddenly become a bit more friendly and eyes seem to catch fire quite a bit more readily as the path they have trail blazed becomes a landing place for others to follow.

---

19 Eckhardt, John http://www.charismamag.com/spirit/prayer/17155-understanding-the-role-of-a-watchman

FORERUNNER:

Forerunning is not an easy task. It is for those who are diligent in seeking the Lord. Like the tribe of Issachar, who understood the times and seasons and what Israel ought to do, 1 Chronicles 12:32, they guard and help direct the work of the entire body. In the wilderness travels of Israel, Issachar was uniquely positioned and grouped with Judah and Zebulon on the East side of the camp. The positioning was important. Judah represented praise going forth to war and worship, Issachar came next with ability to see and discern what to do, and Zebulon brought in the supply. Thus, there was both spiritual and physical supply surrounding the tribe of Isaachar enabling them to focus on discerning the times and seasons.

With an incessant desire to continue moving forward and a view towards the future, the road Watchmen forge is much like what pioneers encountered in an untrod wilderness. The walk is not easy and can be riddled with embedded old thick roots or boulders that block the pathway. These obstacles can frequently represent mindsets of tradition that resist new pioneering efforts. Some of the roots are so thick it takes time to crack through them, and boulders are so big, it requires skill to navigate around them. Such groundbreaking work requires patience. Luke 8:15 promises, "But the ones (seeds) that fell on good ground are those who, having heard the word with a noble and good heart, keep it and bear fruit with patience," Luke 8:15. Hebrews 6:12 exhorts us to "imitate those who through faith and patience inherit the promises."

In our call to our city, we certainly experienced waves of breakthrough, but also seasons of great resistance. Now after nearly seventeen years of plowing and paving the way, we are seeing next generation rise up with the same hunger and desire for more of Him. They are filling the trenches that have spiritually been prepared for them. Relentless in their pursuit, watchmen pave the way waiting for the day when those called behind them see the path and run to it. Such plowing undergirded with patience eventually reaps its reward.

Many of those who have been and are being called into "Watchmen" type ministries are such pioneers. Trailblazing where prayer, particularly corporate expressions were non-existent, they have worked to establish them. These corporate communities are modern day examples of the "ramparts" Habakkuk 2:1 describes. As visionaries, Watchmen function strategically in the body of Christ. They often lend insight into challenges they or others face. They can be found in church boardrooms, businesses, college classrooms, schools, hospital wards, and in every cultural sphere in a community. Because of their stance in the body, they lend insight, timing, and strategy as "Seers."

Forerunners in the worship/prayer movement have already been sent. They have been busy building their worship/prayer communities. Now, however, the season has shifted. Because of the intensity of the times, there is a need to collaborate more effectively. The call of Nehemiah 4:19-20 is real, "The work is great and extensive, and we are separated from one another on the wall. Wherever you hear the sound of the trumpet, rally to us there. Our God will fight for us." Watchmen are being called to 'build the ramparts,' the walkways for communication between various corporate prayer expressions. Such watchmen, hewn in the trenches of the prayer movement, are now pioneering ways to build connections with others. This desire was not present ten years ago to the degree that it is today. The forerunners plowed the ground into which we are now stepping.

In our city, we have held a watch in place since 1998. In July of that year, a "California Call to Prayer" took place. During that convening, Chuck Pierce gave a powerful prophetic word to establish the watch. We took the mandate seriously and have held it in place since then. Though it has distinctly gone through various phases, it has been a tremendous training ground for what we are talking about and walking into now.

In the 'House HOP" ministry outreach to the leadership of our church (mentioned in chapter 6), we heard our pastor say, "They were doing this before anyone else." He said it in such a way that we knew he now understood and received the purpose and message of the gathering. Such is the task of a forerunner. Called by God, you may be sent to areas where you are not well understood, but being faithful to the mission, there comes a day when you can look back on the path you have forged, and see troops begin to land, and God's next phase of His redemptive plan starts to unfold.

STRONG BUILDERS:

One distinctive of a watchman today is their desire and ability to build. There is a unique persona of these builders. Summarizing this characteristic is best relayed in 1 Corinthians 4:15 "For though you might have ten thousand instructors in Christ, yet you do not have many fathers." Reliable builders desire to connect and build with others, a characteristic of fathers (by this I mean mothers as well). Though we are all called to watch, those who are on "active" duty have the ability to work and see how their call, ministry or so called "family" nurtures, works and contributes to others for mutual benefit. This is probably the most distinctive characteristic of a watchman today.

Today's model of a "watch" parallels Nehemiah's wall. Nehemiah set into place people according to their families. Each family had their distinct contribution and culture. However, they were not afraid to work with each other. Each carried their own unique role, none of them overtook, undermined, or imposed limitations on each other. To the contrary, each family's work provided safety and security for another. In building the wall, all were protected. The result was repentance, realignment with

God's covenant law, and revival, "And they stood up in their place and read from the Book of the Law of the Lord their God for one-fourth of the day and for another fourth they confessed and worshiped the Lord their God," Nehemiah 9:3. From this point on, a major transformation began to unfold for Israel. The people re-covenanted with God's laws, Nehemiah 10:28. Most importantly, temple responsibilities were re-instituted through worship and priestly function, Nehemiah 12:45-47.

This picture of rebuilding the wall of Jerusalem is a picture of modern day worship/praise building and connecting across cities, regions, and nations. When watchmen are in place and connected according to their families, God's order is more readily established. 1 Peter 2:5 describes the modern day concept of spiritual wall building, "You also, as living stones, are being built up a spiritual house, a holy priesthood, to offer up spiritual sacrifices acceptable to God through Jesus Christ." His peace abounds and His purpose prospers. Why? Because watchmen are on duty actively called to duty to "Tend and keep" the garden they have been given.

When beginning the process of building the "Global Watch," the Lord spoke to our hearts that there were "Generals in the field, waiting for their marching orders." We have been blessed to meet amazing people who have learned to till their fields, keep watch, and be patient in bearing fruitfulness. They are now ready to connect and know how to build with others. Their attitude is open, searching for the construct to build and connect with other walls and to find families to bridge with. They are the living stones 1 Peter 2:5 speaks of, "You also, as living stones, are being built up a spiritual house, a holy priesthood, to offer up spiritual sacrifices acceptable to God through Jesus Christ." Watchmen are willing to build with carefully tempered mortar. They build desiring none to perish and connecting with other living stones for the express purpose of the Kingdom of God to advance under their watch.

As Watchmen build the ramparts, they do not do it as a momentary job assignment. It requires an ongoing effort. There are both long-term and short-term strategies that arise that will help build the "community" necessary for sustained Kingdom advance. The short-term interventional strategies many times are spurred by what "Watchmen" determine as a necessary alarm, a defensive mobilization. They see trouble coming, sound the alarm, and set up the defenses to guard and protect their constituency. Numbers 10:9 relays this,

> "When you go to war in your land against the enemy who oppresses you, then you shall sound an alarm with the trumpets, and you will be remembered before the Lord your God, and you will be saved from your enemies."

We have seen mobilized target specific prayer intervene strategically on a number of levels, from concern over violent storms, to high-level governmental decisions, to breakthrough strategic prayer over regions, with notable results. One remarkable time, concern was raised over a particular meeting regarding the destiny of Israel and Palestine. Twelve hours of focused prayer towards Israel mobilized 100 intercessors/per hour. Reports rolled out of a violent storm hitting the area where the meeting was taking place. News relayed confusion ruling the meeting followed. No decision was determined from this governmental summit. The enemy assignment was quelled. The intervention was an example of Watchmen mobilizing for a strategic time and purpose. God answered with His distinct and clear affirmation. Interventional strategies may be associated with God's direct answers and signs following, or they may be yet for a time to come. We simply do what God calls us to do, wait for His confirmation and proceed. God does the rest.

As watchmen build and co-labor together, strength will rise that cannot be garnered being separated on the wall. As the communications, and connections develop, the testimony of Jesus will rise creating momentum to carry the mobilization forward. Though the building of the walls and ramparts across the nations is in its early phases now, the fruit of these pioneering connections is already happening. Such testimony breaks barriers for a greater receptivity in the body of Christ. Transformational strength will rise, and as relationships grow, a vibrant, united bride is making herself ready. With such a mobilization, watchmen will surely be placed on the walls of Jerusalem. They will not be silent day or night, Isaiah 62:6-7. The preparations are being made for the "Return of the King."

APPLICATION:

1. Have you forerun anything in your ministry or life? What were the major obstacles? What were the major blessings?
2. Do you have a dream or vision that has not yet come to fulfillment? What do you need to accomplish it? Prioritize your needs. Who has God placed in your sphere of influence and relationships that can assist you with it?
3. When was the last time you simply offered assistance to someone or ministry in need of your gift?

Nine

WATCHMEN AS SEERS: DANIEL'S CRY, WISDOM'S CALL

"The Fear of the Lord is clean."

Psalm 19:9

"Of the sons of Issachar who had understanding of the times, to know what Israel ought to do."

1 Chronicles 14:32

"I was watching and the same horn was making war against the saints, and prevailing against them, until the Ancient of Days came, and a judgment was made in favor of the saints of the Most High, and the time came for the saints to possess the Kingdom."

Daniel 7:21-22

As we face the headwinds of increasingly tumultuous times, discerning life and circumstances through God's eyes will be crucial for every believer. Cultivating the clarity of Watchmen is vital in facing the challenges today. We are in times much like Daniel when both judgment and mercy are walking side by side in the nations. In such an environment, how are we to respond and pray? Discerning God's heart in the midst of the upheavals will be imperative, lest we run to every disaster and find ourselves exhausted in the end. There is a "Daniel's cry" and a "Wisdom's call" rising in the body of Christ. How do we pray for nations in the throws of God's almighty hand of judgment on one hand and mercy on the other. 2 Peter 3:9 promises, "The Lord is not slack concerning His promise, as some count slackness, but is longsuffering towards us, not willing that any should perish but that all should come to repentance?" How do we pray when judgment may be the inciting cause of the upheavals that daily pummel the headlines of our news?

There is an end-time battle for our hearts. Deception threatens to manipulate truth at every turn. Scriptures foretold of the times we now face. In times of increasing lawlessness, Jesus warned in Matthew 24:12, "And because lawlessness will abound the love of many will grow cold." He goes on to say in Matthew 24:24, "For false christs and false prophets will rise and show great signs and wonders to deceive, if possible, even the elect." These are sobering words and warnings with only one answer: Jesus!

Daniel lived in a nation brought into captivity under judgment. In that place, he endured the upheaval and confusion of forced dislocation, navigated through the changes, found his footing, withstood the pressures of a foreign culture and found his place to influence a nation into its deliverance. Lessons from his life hold keys for the days in which we now live. This chapter is not an analysis of end-time eschatology, but rather a review of character to assist us in navigating days of certain change as God moves His mighty hand across the nations to bring His divine plan into place.

DANIEL'S CRY:

In times of both manifestations of God's mercy and His judgment, a very real question now is, how are we to stand and pray? When that question was first posed to me, it made me take a long hard look at how, when, and why I pray. Concerns are flying around daily that could easily drive us into exhaustion. How then should we live? To answer that question, living in a time of both the judgment and the delivering power of God, the character and life of Daniel are worth reviewing. Throughout his life, there was one theme that secured him in the face of the upheavals of his time, a relentless separation and devotion to God. It led to a lifestyle of living under the "Fear of the Lord."

As a key watchman for Israel, Daniel lived through the upheaval of a nation's downfall and captivity. In that place, he was able to navigate the changes in culture and guide an empire with powerful revelatory insight from the Lord. He was thrust into life-threatening situations in both reviled and honored positions. His firm stance before the Lord eventually led to the release and return of the Jews to Israel. What lessons can we learn from his life that can hold us steady in the times we now live?

The first mention of any form of fear in the Bible is in Genesis 3:10. After eating the forbidden fruit of the tree of the knowledge of good and evil, Adam said to God, "I heard Your voice in the garden, and I was *afraid* because I was naked; and I hid myself." The word "afraid" is the Hebrew word "yârê'" meaning to fear morally, to revere, cause to frighten, dread. This word yârê', to fear, first appeared after man's fall. Such an emotion was not present before the fall. That day a line was drawn between the tree of knowledge of good and evil and the tree of life in the garden God intended us to "tend and keep." Fear is the measuring line between whom we serve and what we pursue.

The battle lines were drawn that day in the garden between the "Fear of man," and the "Fear of God." Today, there is an end-time battle for the hearts and minds of men over these two fears. They both continue as strong influences in our lives. "Fear" and what we choose to focus on are a key pivot points in our spiritual walk and journey. Which tree are we drawing from? Are we heading for the tree of the knowledge of good and evil, or to the tree of life? In between the choice is a dividing line that in spiritual terms could be called the ""yârê'" or fear line. In the midst of life's journeys, challenges, decisions, whom do we revere? What drives our decisions? In the demands of today's culture, how do we know we are moving and being motivated by the right things. Daniel understood and lived out the precept of living under the fear of the Lord.

CONFIDENCE:

The fear of the Lord is associated with both knowledge and wisdom. In fact, they are frequently mentioned together. Proverbs 9:10 promises, "The fear of the Lord is the beginning of wisdom, and the knowledge of the Holy One is understanding." These qualities are a powerful combination that produce a quiet confidence in believers. Proverbs 14:26 relays this relationship, "In the fear of the Lord there is strong confidence, and His children will have a place of refuge."

Daniel, in the events leading to being thrown into the lion's den, displayed the "fear of the Lord." He held on to a quiet confidence in the

Lord by not giving into the cultural pressures of the day. When Darius became King, new edicts were signed, inciting significant governmental turmoil and change. In spite of the upheaval, Daniel found favor. Daniel "Distinguished himself above the governors and satraps, because an excellent spirit was in him," Daniel 6:3. Because of the favor given Daniel, powerful governors and satraps became jealous and tried to find fault with him. Under this cloudy environment, Daniel quietly went home, opened his windows to pray three times a day and gave thanks to God. Picture that! A man in the midst of kingdoms in change, with jealous governors and satraps all around him decided to simply kneel and pray. This is an example of living under the fear of the Lord, posed in quiet confidence in the face of life-threatening danger. The jealousy driving the governors and satraps led them to go to King Darius to complain and force his hand to throw Daniel into the lion's den. As they did so, Darius spoke to Daniel, "Your God, whom you serve continually, He will deliver you," Daniel 6:17. Daniel's unrelenting stance to serve and revere the Lord in the face of tremendous cultural opposition saved him and brought him into great favor before the King.

The battle of jealousy and envy surrounding Daniel was a gateway into the next phase of his life. Continually seeking the Lord and not being thwarted by the threats all around him, Daniel survived the critical test of trusting God in the midst of the lion's den. Surviving the test, God opened Daniel's eyes even further. The remaining years of Daniel's life were primarily visionary, speaking about times we live in today. His stance before the Lord opened vistas of revelation for the future in which we still read today. His influence and favor continued in the courts of the Medo-Persian empire and eventually led to the release of the Israelites to go back to Israel and repair the broken walls of Jerusalem.

Today, in the face of headwinds of change, moral and ethical challenge, divisions in the body, the fear of the Lord is a vital stance for all believers to take, particularly if called to the "watchman" position. If we are being driven by anxiety, uncertainty, jealousy, envy we are not operating in the fear of the Lord. We are venturing towards the tree of the knowledge of good and evil, being manipulated by the fear of man. Bitter envies, selfish ambitions, critical words have no root in the tree of life. Proverbs 23:17 exhorts, "Do not let your heart envy sinners, but be zealous for the **fear of the Lord** all the day."

God has given us gifts and callings that are irrevocable. We can have confidence that our gifts and callings are tools God has given us to minister to His body, but the strength in which they are wielded is in the fear of the Lord. Isaiah 11:2 relays this strength, "The Spirit of the Lord shall rest upon Him, the Spirit of wisdom and understanding, the Spirit of counsel and might, the Spirit of knowledge and of the *fear of the Lord*." In the face of tremendous opposition, Daniel was such a man. God gave Him great favor and spiritual insight as a result of his continued reverence in "Fear of the Lord."

SIGHT AND INSIGHT:

From Daniel surviving the lion's den in chapter 6 to the end of the book, wisdom and counsel were displayed through the powerful visions Daniel received from the Lord. How does the "fear of the Lord," give us spiritual sight and insight? Psalm 19:9 states the "Fear of the Lord is clean, enduring forever." Such reverential fear of a holy God cleanses our hearts and is vital for clarity as watchmen face confusing whirlwinds in the future. Clean, from the Hebrew word "Tahor," defines something that is undefiled. It is the word that describes many essential elements in the worship of the Lord in the Old Testament:

- The animals used for Noah's altar were *clean*, in Genesis 8:20.
- It defined the gold that lined the ark of the covenant as *pure*, in Exodus 25:11, the mercy seat in Exodus 25:17.
- The articles of the tabernacle, the dishes, pans, pitches, bowls, were made of *pure* gold in Exodus 25:29.
- The lampstand was made of *pure* gold, Exodus 25:31.
- It describes the incense that will arise from every place in Malachi 1:11, to name a few.
- The words of the Lord are *pure* words, Psalms 12:6.

In other words, the fear of the Lord cleanses us from impurities. It keeps a vibrant, reverential relationship with Jesus in place. Isaiah 11:3 states,

"His delight is in the **fear of the Lord,** and He shall not judge by the sight of His eyes, nor decide by the hearing of His ears, but with righteousness He shall judge the poor, and decide with equity for the meek of the earth."

We have made it a priority in our call to mobilize corporate prayer to always speak life to those around us, particularly in ministry. Divisions happen quickly when the enemy seeks to divide and offend. When the bite of offense takes a hold, all it does is weaken us. How do we know if it is there? Most often such difficulties manifest when quiet confidence and love is not present within us. That is the time to choose like Daniel, to draw back, kneel, pray, and thank God. Bless those who curse you, and seek the Lord until your peace and confidence return. Proverbs 22:4 promises, "By humility and the fear of the Lord are riches and honor and life."

For watchmen, it is vital for our heads to be clear from the subtle grip of manipulation that would bend truth into a self-accomodating or self-promoting place. Such reverential fear and profound trust in the Lord rids us of all the hindrances offenses offer. Respect and reverence for God in His holiness inspires a pure and unadulterated relationship with Jesus to keep our spirit alert and alive in Him.

PERFECTING LOVE:

We cannot understand the fear of the Lord without understanding the nature of who God is. 1 John 4:8 promises, "He who does not love does not know God, for God is love." He is the creator of the universe. In times of increasing deception, we must receive and know God's love. John exhorts the import of cultivating love,

> "Love has been perfected among us in this: that we may have bold-ness in the day of judgment; because as He is, so are we in this world. There is no fear in love; but perfect love casts out fear, because fear involves torment. But he who fears has not been made perfect in love. We love Him because He first loved us." 1 John 4:17-19

The fear mentioned in 1 John 4:18 is the fear of man. God's love has the power to overcome this fear. The challenge in our lives is to develop and mature that love within us to the point of overcoming every setback or scheme the fear of man can impose. The essence of this process is in Deuteronomy 10:12,

> "And now, Israel, what does the Lord your God require of you, but to fear the Lord your God, to walk in all His ways and to love Him,

to serve the Lord your God with all your heart and with all your soul, and to keep the commandments of the Lord and His statutes which I command you today for your good."

God's Word is His covenant. Psalm 18:30 promises, "The Word of the Lord is proven; He is a shield to all who trust in Him." It is above His name, Psalm 138:2. His Word is the solid food that can cultivate and grow His love in our lives. Daniel not only loved God but was a student of the law and obeyed it. As a result, he was sought after for by Persian kings Nebuchadnezzar and Darius. In seeking interpretation of Nebuchadnezzar's dream, in his words, Daniel relayed the import of knowing the laws of the Lord,

"He gives wisdom to the wise and knowledge to those who have understanding. He reveals deep and secret things; He knows what is in the darkness and light dwells with Him. I thank You and praise You, O God of my fathers; You have given me wisdom and might, and have now made known to me what we asked of you." Daniel 2:21-23

Later, in a time of deep revelation, Daniel went into a time of prayer and repentance for what the Lord had shown him. He relayed his respect for the commandments of the Lord, "O Lord, great and awesome God, who keeps His covenant and mercy with those who love Him, and with those who keep His commandments," Daniel 9:4. Daniel's life reflected the balance between love and being rooted in the commandments of God.

In ministry, there is an interweaving of both the Word and the love of God that keeps us on a healthy path, walking towards the "tree of life." When love and the solid footing of His Word are out of balance, we will be out of balance. Spiritual pride from the tree of knowledge of good and evil can easily take over our attitudes. I have learned whenever the critical spirit begins to raise its ugly head, it's time to step back, worship, and love on God. It is in these times of worship and seeking Him; suddenly, the situations begin to reveal a new perspective. Conversely, when direction seems far away, I know it is time to seek His Word. There are times when the Word can overwhelm us with revelation. The revelation will feed our love and conversely, there are times when His Presence can overwhelm us inspiring the revelation of His Word. Such interweaving of His love and His Word leads to a powerful and productive life of love and obedience. That combination in and of itself is a success!

THE WALK OF OBEDIENCE:

The relationship between the love of the Lord and respect for His law is relayed in Psalm 25:14, "The secret of the Lord is with those who fear Him, and He will show them His covenant." What a statement of trust for those who fear Him! The fear of the Lord causes us to love God and revere His Word, His covenant. As we stand in a reverential fear of the Lord, the Lord also trusts us. As we diligently seek Him, God will show us His covenant revealed through His Word. The word "Show" in this scripture is the Hebrew word "Yada" meaning knowledge. By searching out His Word with a heart that truly seeks to understand, God will grant us wisdom and knowledge permeated in His love with reverence in the "fear of the Lord." In fact, the love 1 John 5:3 speaks of is "For this is the love of God, that we keep His commandments. And His commandments are not burdensome." Keeping a balance between both love and the commandments shown in His Word will lead to a life of obedience. What is success? It is a life of simply walking in love and obedience.

The foundational motivation in the watchman response to trials will always be to pursue love and walk in obedience. Our primary pursuit is His

Presence, not our vision, ministry, church, calling, gifts, position, but love. Without love, we will be a noisy gong and clanging symbol, 1 Corinthians 13:1. If love is our goal, the natural result will be a relentless desire to see His Kingdom manifest. We will see the manifestation of God's Word in our lives and circumstances around us. "If you abide in Me, and My words abide in you, you will ask what you desire, and it shall be done for you. **By this My Father is glorified**, that you bear much fruit; so you will be my disciples," John 15: 7-8. Our stance will be aligned with the Lord, and we will be able to fulfill the mandate, "For thus has the Lord said to me: 'Go, set a watchman, let him declare what he sees,'" Isaiah 21:6.

APPLICATION:

1. On a scale of 1-10 (one being lowest) what level of confidence is your walk with the Lord?
2. How can you improve your level of intimacy and trust with the Lord?
3. In your actions, ministry, is love the main driver behind the work and ministry you do?

Ten

Ignite the Night and Awaken the Dawn

"For a thousand years in Your sight are like yesterday
when it is past, and like a watch in the night."

Psalm 90:4

Are you being awakened in the middle of the night? Or wrestled with your thoughts about what happened during the day and lost sleep over it? It may be God calling. Interwoven and somewhat hidden in the pages of scripture is a powerful strategy yielding not only personal encounters with God but powerful corporate breakthrough and Kingdom advance. Prayers and worship during the night hours are incredibly powerful. Luke 12:39 warns, "But know this, that if the master of the house had known what hour the thief would come, he would have watched and not allowed his house to be broken into." There is a significant spiritual activity that occurs in the night season. Thus prayers and seeking the Lord during these hours have a magnified impact. Certainly, all prayers are powerful, but the night season carries a significant weight and is a powerful tool for both personal and corporate spiritual breakthrough and advance.

We tripped upon the power of the night watch shortly after moving to the city where we presently live. As we prepared and moved, we knew God was calling us to pray for the city. We were called to mobilize a prayer conference for California out of concerns for the state. Chuck Pierce gave a powerful prophetic word to establish the "Watches," at the "Call to Prayer." We did just that. In following through and mobilizing prayer for the community, we visited churches and called several ministries. It did not take long for us to realize there was very little established prayer ministry in the churches or the city. Instead, we found six dedicated prayer warriors. We decided to take on the fourth watch of the night, from 3am-6am, with each person taking one night a week. Along with the night prayer assignment, we committed to meet once a week to pray and support each other. The results were incredible. In a city known for its high crime rate, reports came out three months later of the rate dropping by 30%. In fact, at one point, there was no crime reported over a week's period. The news casters found out about our small prayer group and decided to interview us. From that point on, everything else began to erupt. Today, there are numerous active prayer groups throughout the city with some churches developing their prayer ministries. Such activity in prayer was unheard of a decade and a half ago. That experience convinced me that there is significant power in the night watch where a small remnant of people can make a powerful impact.

BIBLICAL FOUNDATIONS:

One of the key ongoing underlying strategies in building the "ramparts" or communities of prayer, is focusing on the night watch, particularly the 4th watch. Jews, Greeks, and Romans, all adopted these military watches during the night hours. In the Hebrew culture (Old Testament terminology), there were three watches, "Beginning of the watches," Lamentations 2:19;

the middle watch, Judges 7:19; and the morning watch, Exodus 14:24; 1 Samuel 11:11.[20]After the establishment of the Roman supremacy (New Testament), the number of watches was increased to four. The first watch was 6pm-9pm; second watch 9pm-12MN, third watch, 12MN-3am, and fourth watch was 3am-6am.[21]

Developing a corporate 4th watch, 3am-6am in a community is a "sync" that people can understand and easily do. It is a point of agreement, a defined space and a key that opens a door through which a "culture of prayer" can develop in any community or environment.

As evidence of the power of the night watch, consider these strategic events that take place particularly during the night and early morning hours/watches:

- Jacob wrestled with God and met Him face to face before receiving his full identity and name as Israel. Genesis 32:22-31
- Moses led the Israelites across the Red Sea. Exodus 14:25-26
- Gideon defeated the Midianites (middle watch). Judges 7:19-24
- The angels appear to the shepherds in the field to announce the birth of the savior. Luke 2:8-14
- Peter and Jesus walk on water. Matthew 14:25-26
- Jesus is resurrected from the dead. Matthew 28:1
- The bridegroom woes His bride in the night hours. Song of Solomon 3:1, Matthew 25:1-13

The events speak for themselves. There is power in meeting with God during the night watch.

---

20 http://biblehub.com/topical/w/watches_of_night.htm
21 http://www.christianity.com/bible/dictionary.php?dict=sbd&id=4446

Furthermore, Jesus cautions that the enemy is quite active in the night season. He warned, "But know this, that if the master of the house had known what hour the thief would come, he would have watched and not allowed his house to be broken into," Luke 12:39. Prayer and worship during these hours do much to intervene upon enemy plans to withhold Kingdom activity during the day. Job 38:12-15 relays the power of prayer during these hours:

"Have you commanded the morning since your days began, and caused the dawn to know its place, that it might take hold of the ends of the earth, and the wicked be shaken out of it? It takes on form like clay under a seal, and stands out like a garment. From the wicked their light is withheld, and the upraised arm is broken."

In other words, prayers during these hours do much to command what happens during the day. Want to have a particularly productive day, or have important things to do during the day? Try praying during these hours and see how God's plans unfold before your eyes.

THE IMPORT OF THE NIGHT WATCH:

In many communities the culture of prayer is not very well developed. Many churches, even today, do not have identified prayer ministries. They may have people who pray, but by and large, prayer ministries are not well developed. As a result, communities are frequently divided and the "spiritual" ground quite difficult to navigate. A culture of prayer simply is not present. This is not a condemnation on communities/cities/regions, but is merely an observation. It may be an overt expression of a "stronghold" over regions, a spiritual power/principality that keeps people captured under its influence. 2 Corinthians 10:3-5 speaks of this,

"For though we walk in the flesh, we do not war according to the flesh. For the weapons of our warfare are not carnal but mighty in God for pulling down strongholds, casting down arguments and every high thing that exalts itself against the knowledge of God, bringing every thought into captivity to the obedience of Christ."

The 4th watch is a strategic key for watchmen as significant Kingdom advance can be harnessed with a small remnant of committed people. Why? Praying during these hours, particularly in corporate agreement, carries a great weight spiritually. Psalm 90:4 declares the power of prayers in the night season, "For a thousand years in Your sight are like yesterday when it is past, and like a watch in the night." Prayers in the night carry the weight of days and years propelling them as a contending force forward. Strongholds that keep a culture of prayer from rising and people separated, as well as other issues locked in over regions, i.e. lawlessness, crime, drug addictions, poverty, etc., are significantly impacted with prayer intervention during these hours.

For those in the USA, the 4th watch and the night watch carries destiny for our nation. On October 12, 1565, Jean Ribault, a French Hugonaut, recited Psalm 132 over our nation on the shores of present-day Jacksonville, Florida just before being impaled by Spanish conquistadors. Psalm 132:3-5 relays prophetic destiny for the night watch in America:

"Surely I will not go into the chamber of my bed; I will not give sleep to my eyes, or slumber to my eyelids, until I find a place for the Lord a dwelling place for the Mighty one of Jacob," Psalm 132:3-5

However, America is not to be singled out. The call is for all. Proverbs 1:28 states, "Those who seek me diligently will find me." The word diligently is the Hebrew word šâḥar, meaning early at any task, to rise and seek early. Seeking through worship and prayer during these hours carries significant spiritual weight. Furthermore, God is doing it. He is waking His body up to become His bride.

The night watch ignited and even sustained significant revivals in the past. The outpouring in Herrnhut began with youth praying and singing through the city streets in the night. "Several groups called 'bands' had already started doing 'nightwatch' prayer meetings by themselves, in which they would walk singing through the village.[22] It was from these night watches the revelation of unceasing prayer/worship sprang.

When I have had the opportunity to speak about the night watch, invariably 50-75% of the audiences raise their hands admitting being wakened during the night hours. It is time for us, the body of Christ, to be like Samuel. Once Samuel figured out it was the Lord calling, his response was, "Speak, for your servant hears." How much Kingdom advance we would see if we, the body of Christ, would respond similarly to His call! If God is calling, rise, worship, and pray and see the enemy pushed back and His Kingdom advance during the day.

THE 4TH WATCH AND BEYOND:

The fourth watch is not the end. It is just the beginning. When we initiated the "watch" in our region, it was a city that was divided with few identifiable prayer ministries. The "Watch" has now been in existence over the past 18 years. Though it has gone through various phases of development, it has not stopped. We are on the verge of moving into a new wave of another season.

---

22 https://yearningheartsjourney.blogspot.com/2011/06/zinzendorf-moravian-revival-and.html

It is a mistake to "silo" thinking that the watch is only about the 4th watch. If we do this, we will miss the transformational impact the "Watch" has for the communities in which we live and work. The spiritual "loosening" over a region will declare itself with transformational evidence in our daily lives. The spiritual impact of prayer, particularly the night watch, may emerge through crime rates plummeting, healings, reconciliation, or political, social, or environmental changes that align with Kingdom dynamics. In his work on transformation George Otis notes, "Persevering leadership and united prayer are present in all of our transformation case studies.[23]" Kingdom advance through transformation will always manifest with the testimony of Jesus rising. When this "loosening" occurs, it's time to look up, seek His face diligently for the next step. When it is clear, take the advance. Your prayers are working, and it's time to move forward.

APPLICATION:

1. Are you being wakened in the middle of the night? If so, how often?
2. How might waking to pray/worship in the middle of the night change your walk with the Lord?
3. What could you do to mobilize or participate in more coordinated prayer in the night season for your community or city?

---

23 http://www.ijfm.org/PDFs_IJFM/15_4_PDFs/06%20Otis%20Second.pdf

Eleven

BUILDING A CULTURE OF PRAYER AND COMMUNITY FOR TRANSFORMATION AND REVIVAL

"That in the dispensation of the fullness of the times He might gather together in one all things in Christ, both which are in heaven and which are on earth—in Him."

Ephesians 1:10

Groups of two, three, dozens, whatever the culture supplies, are meeting to seek the Lord and hear from Him directly. Such is the "Encounter" culture of a remnant rising across the nations at this hour. It is a "Grassroots" call from heaven itself. People are gathering daily, or at the very least regularly, for the sole purpose of hearing from the Lord and being in His Presence. Experiencing the promise of Deuteronomy 4:29, "But from there you will seek the Lord your God, and you will find Him if you seek Him with all your heart and with all your soul," their hunger drives them and the escalating times spur them. Ephesians 1:10 speaks of this time, "that in the dispensation of the fullness of the times He might gather together in one all things in Christ, both which are in heaven and which are on earth—in Him."

As people respond to this call, their vision shifts from their personal wants and needs to their neighborhood and on to the nations. We are in a time when God desires to connect the "Grassroots" of our cities, states, regions, and nations. As the root systems intertwine, the harvest fields become robust and mature. Preparation is underway to gather the "wheat," and bring it into the barn for the end time harvest of nations. As times intensify, a God inspired desire is rising in the body of Christ to more jointly work together. Jesus prophesied of the end time harvest emerging when both the tares and the wheat are mature. In Matthew 13:30 Jesus exhorts, "Let both grow together until the harvest, and at the time of harvest I will say to the reapers, "First gather together the tares and bind them in bundles to burn them, but gather the wheat into my barn."" How will the wheat be gathered? The wheat will be gathered by building the bridges through meaningful and intentional relationships with those who consistently meet to worship/pray and encounter God. The word "Encounter," says it all regarding the call of Watchmen to build their communities and culture of prayer. Such focus in houses of prayer, churches, prayer groups will lead to transformation of individuals and communities fueling the fire for revival.

THE TESTIMONY:

As watchmen gather across the nations to build their "ramparts" or communities of prayer, each will have their distinct flavor, personality, and way of doing things. Underlying each corporate prayer expression are specific principles that are based and threaded through Scripture. Two threads carry significant value in the transformation of communities, one of relentless corporate worship/prayer focused on *encountering* God through "Bridal intercession," and second, target specific prayer.

Today, the same principles apply. Both consistent ongoing corporate "encounter" driven prayer and target specific prayer carry spiritual weight with transformational impact.

Example 1: The call came a few days before Christmas. On the other end of the line was our pastor who excitedly relayed the news of an entire mall in the center of our city being donated to the church. He was inviting us to take a look. My husband looked at me in utter amazement as he put the phone down relaying the facts of the conversation. None of us could believe a massive 165,000 square foot, well-constructed, building would simply be handed over to a church...in the center of the city, with ample parking and city lights to boot! Within a few days of the call, the keys to the building, a 165,000 square foot structure, sitting dormant for years, was suddenly released to serve the city. Plans unfolded, and renovation immediately began for a "city center," a center committed to serving the public. None of us could believe the generosity of the gift. The potential to serve the community was unprecedented and continues to unfold.

Hidden elsewhere in the city was a small group of relentless "Watchmen." Holding their ground for over 16 years, they had been faithful and consistent believing for a move of God to transform the city. Their assignment was to seek the Lord, find Him, and declare what they see. It is and has been a "Presence-Encounter" driven gathering that has continued to draw people through to this day. Though the "watch" had been through various phases, it had not relented nor given up. It had maintained its primary goal which was to "watch, and pray" and continues to this day, now seeing the manifestation of years of "standing in the gap," become a foundational part of a transformational vehicle in a community.

Example 2: In response to a sense of urgency for the USA, a convening was mobilized with representatives from across the Western Coast to seek the Lord for the sake of the nation. The "Trumpet Call West Coast" was held one year before a national election. Facilitators met for a day and a half ahead of the general convening to strategize steps going forward. Through much prayer and seeking the Lord together, a decision was made to carry forward a vision to establish prayer during the 4th watch along the Western Coast of America, Alaska to Southern California. Throughout the gatherings, there was a joining of hearts, deep repentance, and humility amongst participants. A real sense of family arose. As a result, sessions were met with a powerful Presence of the Lord. Vision and purpose towards a 4th watch (prayer from 3am-6am) were cast and mobilized along the Western Coast of America.

During the weeks of preparation, the Lord spoke to my heart that He would respond much as He did in Exodus 19 with thunder, lightning, and rain. Exodus 19:13 is the first mention of "trumpet" in the Bible. In this chapter, Moses was commanded to call all Israel together at Mount Sinai. On the third day, He would descend to meet with them. As we were in one of the deepest and longest droughts on earth, I did not have faith to speak out what the Lord had spoken. Furthermore, we were in the middle of a scalding summer in which rain never happens.

On the third day of the meeting, God responded powerfully. Two hours after the meeting ended, we were met with thunder, lightning, rain and hail as an unpredicted display of the Lord of

Hosts erupted. A massive, record-breaking storm hit the state from north to south extending into the NW states. The storm came out of nowhere. "God thunders marvelously with His voice," (Job 37:5). Let there be no mistake...there is a God in heaven who hears and responds to our cries. Rain fell in record quantities in Los Angeles, beating previous July records set in 1886. Two inches of hail dumped on northern CA highways including Lake Tahoe. Nearly two inches of rain fell in San Diego, and an outpouring in the Mojave Desert...in July, the hottest, driest month of the year and the midst of a record-breaking drought.

Headlines in the Bakersfield Californian the following day were "Climate Change!" Though not directly related to the rainfall, it was a prophetic message. Los Angeles times followed with headlines declaring, "Weird Weather." It was a distinct moment in time for a spiritual breakthrough from which a significant mobilization of watchmen arose to take their place in building the prayer wall for America. The Lord of Hosts showed up with undeniable signs of His affirmation. He also stamped the confirmation of the call to "Watch" with His supernatural intervention. As a remnant from across the America got word, the "Watch" spread through the time zones of the USA and into other nations. It was a spiritual, profound breakthrough moment in time when God set His divine purposes in order. Only God could do such a thing. That convening, that strategic, breakthrough moment in time when God showed His divine confirmation, was, in part, the impetus for this book.

The above are contrasting examples of "watchman" prayers and functions today. The first relays the import of sustained, relentless prayer in community, and the second, the impact of focused, time specific, strategic, breakthrough prayers.

The past season of the prayer movement has been graced through the revelation and power of "Bridal intercession." Much has been written about this search for intimacy in worship/prayer through unceasing praise and worship. The powerful ministry and influence of IHOP Kansas City and other prayer hubs in the nations have led the way to this God inspired culture of prayer. Such prayer/worship has been a valued and important part of God's plan in preparation for His return. The Biblical foundations are reflected in a number of scriptures most notably Amos 9:11 and Acts 15:16-17. James exhorts the disciples at the Jerusalem Council of the church's prophetic call to unceasing prayer in the spirit of the Tabernacle of David in Acts 15:16-17,

"After this I will return and will rebuild the tabernacle of David, which has fallen down; I will rebuild its ruins, and I will set it up; so that the rest of mankind may seek the Lord, even all the Gentiles who are called by My name, says the Lord who does all these things."

We don't know if the tabernacle David set up was 24/7 or morning and evening. 1 Chronicles 16:40 says priests were set in place "To offer burnt offerings to the Lord on the altar of burnt offering regularly morning and evening." Given the large number of instruments and people participating, it was likely 24/7. (1 Chronicles 6:31-48; 1 Chronicles 15:16-24; 1 Chronicles 25:1-31)

Of note, once the tabernacle was established by David, 1 Chronicles 18-20 relay the conquests of Israel. The Philistines, Moab, Edom, Ammon, Rabbah were all defeated. The Syrians who assisted Hadadezer, King of Zobah, were also defeated and became servants of David bringing him tribute, 1 Chronicles 18:6. These testimonies of victory relay the impact of unceasing worship and prayer penetrating the spiritual atmosphere and releasing the supply line of heaven. Through worship/prayer, the "heaven's declare the glory of God."

Through the watchman call, bridal intercession will take on a new level of meaning as focus develops not only towards personal worship to God, but an added desire and focus on "Encountering" God and listening to His voice, hearing His word and instructions. It is a subtle but purposeful shift. It does not deny the giving of our praise and worship or belittle "bridal intercession," but rather adds to it. The biblical picture is of Jacob, who would not let go of God until He blessed him, Genesis 32:22-32. Such an "Encounter" driven desire will be increasingly necessary to face the challenges ahead.

DYNAMIC DUO:

There is a power dynamic between the duo of Bridal/Encounter driven intercession interacting with strategic, targeted prayer. Focused prayer has an identifiable, often measurable influence upon a community and will have a scriptural purpose in addressing. Ongoing prayer provides a foundational spiritual atmosphere for Kingdom advance and is often the birthplace for more strategic interventional prayer. The two forms can in many ways be viewed in the natural much like the military. The broader military forces lay a foundation of military protection while the special ops go in to break through strategic strongholds or targets. Both require information, but the strategy is quite different. The broader military is mobilized for the more general advance and the special ops for specific focused release of strongholds. The difference is that strategic, targeted, informed intercession takes place often over a shorter period with the undergirding of ongoing corporate worship and prayer. Both forms are always redemptive in nature. In other words, the purpose of the target is to release the grip of the enemy and redeem the value and destiny of God over a particular target or region.

It does not take masses to make a difference. Not only are the large formed networks, houses of prayer, large event oriented gatherings important, God is now looking for the two by two's, the small groups hidden in homes diligently and regularly praying in unceasing praise. They represent the "Grassroots" of the prayer movement and will be vital for any sustained transformation or revival coming down the spiritual pipeline. These small contending forces are just as valued as the large events and formed prayer hubs and houses of prayer. All are needed. Matthew 18: 20 promises, "For where two or three are gathered together in My name, I am there in the midst of them." The power and discipline of committed corporate unrelenting prayer is the spear that breaks through the heavens.

From ongoing "Encounter" inspired intercession comes revelation for the strategic point focused assignments of the watchman call. Countless prayer journeys are birthed in the prayer rooms of corporate intercession. Being sent from the throne room of heaven, these target specific assignments break through cultural barriers paving the way for Kingdom advance. The above example is one of many targeted times of strategic prayer intervening for specific time related purpose yielding tremendous advance for His Kingdom.

Consistent, contending, communities of worship and prayer combined with strategic breakthrough prayer are foundation stones for revivals in the past and will be for the future. Jesus is coming for an alert, passionate, alive, and awakened bride. The spiritual hunger inspired through "Encounter" driven prayer will play a significant role in preparing people for the days we see approaching. Hebrews 10:24-25 states, "And let us consider one another in order to stir up love and good works, not forsaking the assembling of ourselves together, as is the manner of some but exhorting one another, and so much the more as you see the Day approaching."

BIBLICAL FOUNDATIONS:

A scriptural version of both ceaseless and strategic targeted worship/prayer working together is in 2 Chronicles 34. After almost 100 years had passed since Hezekiah's reform, Josiah came to rule in Judah. The northern kingdom had already been taken into captivity. It was a nation that had relapsed into idolatry, precariously hanging in the balance having lost its spiritual compass. When he came to rule, Josiah was six years old. At the tender age of 14, he dedicated time to seek the Lord for the nation. It is a picture of purposeful intercession for a nation that was astray. He took four years to seek the Lord. 2 Chronicles 34:2 relays,

> "For in the eighth year of his reign (age 14), while he was still young, he began to seek the God of his father, David, and in the twelfth year (age 18) he began to purge Judah and Jerusalem of the high places, the wooden images, the carved images, and the molded images immediately broke down the altars of Baal."

Josiah knew the condition of the nation, saw what was happening and spent time seeking the Lord, finding Him and His heart for the strategy to begin a transformational process for the nation. Such searching could be characterized by intentional worship to "Encounter" God. This is an example relentless, "Encounter" driven intercession. Note there were twelve years of seeking the Lord before reform began.

From these foundational years of ceaseless, consistent prayer, a remarkable series of events unfolded. In the eighteenth year of Josiah's reign (note how long this took), during the repair of the temple, Hilkiah the high priest, found a most significant part of Israel's history, Moses' book of the law. 2 Chronicles 34:14 states, "Now when they brought out the money that was brought into the house of the Lord, Hilkiah, the priest, found the Book of the Law of the Lord given by Moses." The money and the book were handled with great integrity by the overseers, the Watchmen. Shaphan brought the book to Josiah and read it. Josiah immediately reacted by tearing his robe in an act of repentance for a nation gone astray. "Thus it happened, when the king heard the words of the Law, that he tore his clothes," 2 Chronicles 34:19. Not acting rashly, but in repentance, he sent the priests to a prophetess Huldah to seek the Lord as to what to do. 2 Chronicles 24-28 relays the power of repentance through informed intercession:

"Thus says the Lord: 'Behold, I will bring calamity on this place and on its inhabitants, all the curses that are written in the book which they have read before the king of Judah, because they have forsaken Me and burned incense to other gods, that they might provoke Me to anger with all the works of their hands. Therefore My wrath will be poured out on this place, and not be quenched. But as for the king of Judah, who sent you to inquire of the Lord, in this manner you shall speak to him, 'Thus says the Lord God of Israel: 'Concerning the words which you have heard— because your heart was tender, and you humbled yourself before God when you heard His words against this place and against its inhabitants, and you humbled yourself before Me, and you tore your clothes and wept before Me, I also have heard you,' says the Lord. 'Surely I will gather you to your fathers, and you shall be gathered to your grave in peace, and your eyes shall not see all the calamity which I will bring on this place and its inhabitants.' So they brought back word to the king."

The next step was the restoration of temple worship, unceasing prayer/worship, and reinstitution of the Passover. Talk about a transformational shift! All this was done through purposeful, continuous seeking of the Lord, finding His heart, and following through with His instructions. Josiah called the people to take a stand for righteousness, "And he made all who were present in Jerusalem and Benjamin take a stand, so the inhabitants of Jerusalem did according to the covenant of God, the God of their fathers," 2 Chronicles 31:32. Josiah not only acted as a King but as a Watchman watching over and restoring God's covenant purpose for Israel and Judah.

Furthermore, the story is interesting in that it takes place in Jerusalem with the tribe of Benjamin. Redemption is the key theme for the tribe of Benjamin. When Benjamin was born, Rachel called him Ben-oni,"son of my sorrow " but when she died, Jacob re-named him Benjamin, "Son of my right hand." Their land, though shrouded in horrific abuse and death of the Levite concubine, would ultimately be the place where the events redeeming the world would take place, Jesus' death and resurrection. It is also where the nations of the earth will come to worship the Lord of Hosts on the Feast of Tabernacles during Jesus' rule and reign on earth, Zechariah 14:16.

THE INNER WORKINGS OF A CLOCK:

In reality, how does this concept of a "Watch" and "Watchman" work together? Though prayer unites the church, a "Watch" unites prayer collaborating various prayer visions and assignments together like "clockwork." If you picture the inner workings of a clock and the gears that keep it ticking, the gears are of various sizes. Some run faster than others, but they all carry their unique characteristics and responsibility in keeping the clock ticking. Such is a picture of a "Watch" that has been described throughout this book. The varied sizes and internal shapes of the gears represent the varied assignments and size of prayer ministries involved. The varied characteristics of the wheels can be a picture of the numerous prayer/worship "assignments," i.e. government, media, education, family, or varied sizes of cities/regions connected through a "watch." The center, pinions, of each wheel represents the leadership of a corporate prayer expression, church, HOP, giving momentum to the gear. The outer cogs, represent those intentionally connecting and interacting with other gears.

In the construction of a watch, there are varied sizes and shapes of gears, each carry their weight in making the clock tick. The cogs of each gear fit to help turn the neighboring wheel. In fact, if the smallest wheel stops functioning the entire system can be slowed down if not halted. Such interactive turning is a picture of the import and impact of the night watch, particularly the 4th watch. It can be represented as the smallest gear and functions to keep many of the larger hubs ticking. The 4th watch is a vital biblical and strategic gear to initiate and maintain the building of a watch. Being highly effectual with a small group of people, much can be accomplished spiritually to break open strongholds over cities, regions, even nations during these hours. Revivals historically have begun with focused intercession in the night seasons, as we have seen in the previous chapter. Food for thought when contemplating how to start building a watch, particularly with myriads of other prayer groups, ministries around. It is a unique way of connecting such streams in a non-threatening power-filled strategy.

Why do we need to work together? Because we are more powerful together than separated. The escalating and intensifying times we now face are calling for stronger cohesiveness in prayer. How do we work together? Through intentional relationship. It is that simple. Working in cohesiveness does not mean that every prayer ministry will be involved in a watch. A watch's distinctive has a core value of not only the "assignment" but places a high value on the import of relationship and willingness to work together.

It means that those willing to work intentionally as a watch will do so. Such collaboration is also biblical. Ezekiel 1:16 describes this inner-working, "The appearance of the wheels and their workings was like the color of beryl, and all four had the same likeness. The appearance of their workings was, as it were, a wheel in the middle of a wheel." This is a biblical description of intentional linkage of a "Watch."

Practically speaking, a "Watch" forms when those willing to relate simply do that. Sharing of insights and vision begins the process of finding common connection. The input between the various prayer streams or churches involved sharpens each other by sharing essential information for both strategic target specific prayer and unrelenting corporate expressions. Assignments are not interfered with, but rather passed on to each other and deepened through the efforts. In our city, the foundation of the prayer room for ongoing regular prayer is fed through connection to other streams, ministries, and churches and vice versa. We are very much connected relationally with a group involved in governmental prayer, and with national and international streams of prayer. Such connection alerts us to key issues going on in our city, state and nation. This kind of collaboration can spread to other networks involved in media, education, military, etc. as relationships develop and communication patterns strengthen. As these inner workings of a clock begin to tick and work together, the gears are not harmed or broken, but rather propelled forward through their inner workings.

A lesson in such teamwork is how the Navy SEALs work. Their entire training is centered around team work. The training involved is probably the most difficult military training in the world. The exercises and military rotations required challenge their individual physical and mental capacities to the max. However, throughout their training, they are cautioned it is about "The team." They train as a team. Each with their individual talents and abilities contributes to an entire team effort. Does such teamwork de-value their individual vision, calling, or abilities. No! They work and contribute to one another's strengths. There are countless stories from training and on the field, how one person's strength helps another out of a difficult situation. In the end, the entire team wins. At the end of a SEAL graduation it is said, "Now your watch begins!"

The goal of the watch is the transforming power of His Presence. He is the God of breakthrough and will release His transforming power and strategies as we diligently seek Him. With the great commandments in operation, a vessel for His habitation is formed and we will witness His love in action.

FULLNESS OF THE GENTILE CHURCH AND THE CALL TO EKKLESIA:

Today, preparations are being made for the fullness of the Gentile church and a great end-time harvest. Romans 11:25 is underway,

> "For I do not desire, brethren, that you should be ignorant of this mystery, lest you should be wise in your own opinion, that blindness in part has happened to Israel until the fullness of the Gentiles has come in."

As the wheat field (body of Christ) matures, heads are bowing; they are turning away from the tares of the past and the fullness of the Gentile church is coming in. The hour is upon us to "Watch." The awakening has started. The call to watchmen is intensifying and the remnant is rising. Throughout the earth, as watchmen take their place, the testimony of Jesus is paving the way for an end time harvest. Revelation 4:1 is at the door:

> "After these things I looked, and behold, a door standing open in heaven. And the first voice which I heard was like a trumpet

speaking with me, saying, "Come up here, and I will show you things which must take place after this."

As watchmen respond, the heavens declare, "And the Spirit and the bride say, 'Come!' And let him who hears say, 'Come!' And let him who thirsts come. Whoever desires, let him take the water of life freely," Revelation 22:17. Watchmen, rise and build! The preparation for His return is underway.

APPLICATION:

1. What are your strengths and weaknesses in your personal walk with the Lord?
2. What activity and what hindrances are there in corporate prayer in your community?
3. What steps could you take to participate or mobilize corporate prayer in your community?

Twelve

EKKLESIA NOW, BY
PASTOR GREG SIMAS

"And I also say to you that you are Peter, and on
this rock I will build My church, and the gates of
Hades shall not prevail against it."

Matthew 16:18

When we realize what Jesus actually said regarding the "church" in
Matthew 16, we discover the revelation that what He wants to build
will require personal prayer, corporate prayer, and prophetic intercession as
the primary functional identity of His church. For too long the corporate
prayer meeting has been relegated to the corner of our church bulletins and
buildings and handed off to a small group of "intercessors" in the church.

Prayer must move from the fringes of church programming to the center of church life. Today, you can build a "church" without much prayer,
but you cannot build the Ekklesia without prayer being squarely the center
of all it does.

As we will soon discover, the primary functional identity of the church
is not merely good teaching, flashy gatherings, pastoral care, and warm fellowship but rather to legislate and administrate heaven through corporate

intercession on behalf of cities, regions, and nations until heaven's government is established here on Earth.

I urge you to read this chapter with your heart wide open to the Holy Spirit's revelation on what our Lord is saying to the church, His Ekklesia.

THE GREATEST REVELATION IN THE SPIRITUALLY DARKEST REGION:

In Matthew 16, Jesus and his young disciples make their way north of Jerusalem to the region of Caesarea Philippi. After arriving in Caesarea Philippi, they then take a two-day journey to the region to the Gates of Hades (Hell).

It's here, in Matthew 16:13–18, that the greatest revelation of Jesus as the Christ is made, and with it, His promise to build His church:

"When Jesus came to the region of Caesarea Philippi, he asked his disciples, 'Who do people say the Son of Man is?' They replied, 'Some say John the Baptist; others say Elijah; and still others, Jeremiah or one of the prophets.' 'But what about you?' he asked. 'Who do you say I am?' Simon Peter answered, 'You are the Christ, the Son of the living God.' Jesus replied, 'Blessed are you, Simon son of Jonah, for this was not revealed to you by flesh and blood, but by my Father in heaven. And I tell you that you are Peter, and upon this rock I will build my church, and the gates of Hades will not overcome it.'"

THE REGION OF CAESAREA PHILIPPI:

The region of Caesarea Philippi was the seedbed for occult and idol worship. No devout Jew entered this region due to the spiritual darkness that permeated it.

The Gates of Hades itself sat as a cave at the bottom of Mt. Hermon. Shrines to the goat-man Pan, Caesar, and Nemesis (as well as up to ten others) were visible, along with the practices of temple prostitution, pagan worship, and ritualistic sacrifice. Compare this region to the likes of San Francisco, Las Vegas, and New Orleans all rolled into one.

THE REVELATION OF JESUS AS THE CHRIST:

It's actually at this very place and before these very gates that Jesus confirms Peter's confession that He is the Christ, and our assignment is to build His Church. In Matthew 16:16,18 Simon Peter answered, *"You are the Christ, the Son of the living God,"* verse16. *"And I tell you that you are Peter, and upon this rock I will build my church, and the gates of Hades will not overcome it,"* verse 18.

It's almost shocking to realize that, in the darkest spiritual place on earth, Jesus chooses to give the greatest revelation of who He is. Why not release the revelation in the safety, security, and glory of the temple at Jerusalem? Why here? It is because the revelation of Jesus as the Christ at the Gates of Hades carries our Kingdom assignment, namely, to engage the powers of darkness and bring the saving knowledge of Jesus to all the world. It's at these gates that Jesus chooses to release the full weight of the revelation, namely, that He is the Christ and that it is our mission to partner with him to build the church.

JESUS WANTS TO BUILD:

The revelation made known to Peter and the other disciples comes with a commission. Matthew 16:18 "And I tell you that you are Peter, and upon this rock, I will build my church, and the gates of Hades will not overcome it." If Jesus wants to build something, it is imperative for every believer to know what that something is. If we misinterpret what Jesus intends to build, we are in grave danger of missing both our heavenly mission and our assignment. Our time, energy, and resources will go into building something He never authorized. We end up investing everything into something that was never mandated.

I WILL BUILD MY "CHURCH!"

It is at the Gates of Hades that Jesus releases both the mission and the agency to accomplish the mission. The mission is to destroy the works of darkness at and through the Gates of Hades. The agency Jesus chooses is NOT the church but rather the Ekklesia!

Now, before you stone me, let me explain. The word "church" (Greek word "kuriakon") did not exist until the fourth century, or 300 AD. The closest rendering for the word "church" is from the medieval Greek "kuriakon" and means "the Lord's house." The truth is, the disciples never heard of the word "kuriakon" because the word was not in existence. If Jesus really did say, "I will build my church (kuriakon), and the gates of Hades will not overcome it," the disciples would have looked at Jesus, looked at each other, and then looked back at Jesus and said, "Did you say 'kuriakon'?" What's a kuriakon?" They wouldn't know because the word didn't exist.

Pick a dictionary, any dictionary, and look up the word "church." You will not find the Greek word. Jesus did not use "kuriakon" but rather the word "Ekklesia." The word "kuriakon" or "church" refers to a meeting, a number of believers, or a building. This is not what Jesus said in Matthew 16:18. Have you ever heard or caught yourself asking the following:

- "How was church, today?",
- "Where is your church located?", or
- "How big is your church?"

Our current interpretation of the word "church" has gravely weakened the commission and has turned our mission into something that our Lord never intended we work towards. Is our current understanding of "church" the agency Jesus chose when he stood with his disciples in the darkest, vilest, most demon-infested region on Earth, before the gates of Hades and all of Hell itself? Do you think that our Lord experienced the thirty-nine lashes on his back, the crown of thorns on his head, the brutality of the cross, and His glorious resurrection, so we can build buildings, have good meetings, and call it church? There has to be more!

HOW DID WE GET HERE?'

We have to take a brief trip back through history to uncover where we adopted the word "church" over the word "Ekklesia." The point of this section is to provide a fly-by of historical events that led us away from Christ's original intent, causing us to misunderstand and misappropriate our assignment, impacting both our functional identity and our mission. By shedding light on this, I hope to achieve a "wake-up call" to the body of Christ, and an intentional realignment of our Lord's original assignment with the purpose of getting back on track with what the Lord wants to do on Earth.

- In 325 AD, Roman emperor Constantine (whom it has been said, became a Christian), legalized Christianity. Great cathedrals were built during this time.
- In 380 AD, Theodosius made Christianity the state religion/national religion.
- For over 1,000 years, only the professional clergy, wealthy, and educated who understood Hebrew, Greek, and Latin, had access to the scriptures.

- In 1525 AD, William Tyndale translates the New Testament from Greek to English. The translation is called the "Tyndale Translation."
- Tyndale rightly translates "Ekklesia" as "congregation" in Matt. 16:18: "I will build my congregation..."
- This proper use of the word suddenly creates a potential split in power between the Roman Catholic Church and the Church of England.
- Rome claims that Peter started the "Church"; thus, the Church is to be led by popes and bishops and not placed in the hands of any "congregation."
- Tyndale's accurate translation of this ONE word puts the entire papal system in jeopardy.
- Because Tyndale's translation would become public, the correct translation of Matt. 16:18 would be read by the masses and present a real threat to the power structure of the religious institution.
- Though threatened by the religious system, Tyndale would not rescind the word "congregation." As a result, he was betrayed, sentenced by Thomas More, and burned at the stake in 1536.
- Under the rule of Henry VIII, the Great Bible is produced (1535 AD). This version is, in essence, a rebranded version of the Tyndale Bible, produced to sidestep the papal system after Henry VIII had not been granted permission to divorce his wife and marry another woman. King Henry VIII persuades the English Parliament to separate from the Roman Catholic Church. The 1534 Act of Supremacy makes Henry VIII head of the English Church and officially nullifies the Pope's authority in that country.
- The church at Geneva, Switzerland, produces the Protestant "Geneva Bible" in 1560 AD.

- Under the rule of Queen Elizabeth I, the Bishops Bible is produced in (1568 AD).
- In 1604 AD, a new translation project is started, i.e. "The King James Authorized Version of the Bible" by the now state-run Anglican Church under the rule of King James. The King James version is produced for the English state-run nationalized church to compete with the Protestant Geneva Bible.
- King James deploys 47 translators for the project and issues 15 rules for translation. Within the 15 rules of translation, article 3 says, "The old Ecclesiastical Words to be kept, viz. the Word "church" not be translated congregation."
- By translating Ekklesia as "church" instead of "congregation" or "assembly," King James and the Anglican state church accomplish their goal of maintaining power by defining Christ's body as "the Lord's house" instead of "legislative, ruling assembly."
- The King James Authorized Version quickly grows in popularity and overtakes the Geneva Bible, and with it, the misappropriation of the word Ekklesia as "church" instead of "congregation/ assembly."

The King James Version has been, and still is, THE most popular and number-one-selling translation of the Bible for over 500 years. For 500 years, we've been building the "church" as it's been translated and understood but not building the Ekklesia whom Jesus commissioned. Because "church" and "Ekklesia" carry two different meanings, they bring us different results.

This is why our churches have ceased being apostolic and have become largely pastoral. We measure success by attendance and not influence. Pastors and church leaders feel compelled to keep the "church" plates spinning to fulfill what's been determined as a successful ministry. This is driving pastors and leaders to the brink of godless competition, joyless exhaustion, and career-ending depression, not to mention creating a lack of Kingdom expansion in cities, regions, and nations.

Jesus never commissioned us to sit within the walls of buildings and "do" church but to engage with culture as the Ekklesia. The Church (Ekklesia) was created to take the revelation of Jesus Christ through the Gates of Hades and into the darkest places on Earth.

We must realign ourselves with the original mandate. We must uncover Christ's original intent. We need to rediscover what "Ekklesia" is and shift our priorities accordingly. When we do this, we can truly have a 'Kingdom mindset.'

WHAT IS THE EKKLESIA?

In the days of Jesus, there were three main institutions in Israel: the Temple, the synagogue, and the Ekklesia. Now, most are familiar with the temple and the synagogue but know very little about the Ekklesia. The temple and the synagogue were religious institutions organized to worship and instruct God's people.

The Ekklesia was not religious but governmental. It was first developed by the Greeks hundreds of years before Christ and modified by the Romans when they took power. Every city had an Ekklesia.

The Ekklesia had expansive authority in determining the affairs of cities and territories. It functioned as a legal ruling assembly of a city gathering forty to fifty times a year to lead and govern. Ekklesia's were regularly summoned to actively participate in legislation, declare war, make peace, negotiate treaties, make alliances, elect officials, and more. Ekklesia's were made up of men, eighteen years and older, who had served in the military for a minimum of two years.

"In legal co-operation with the Senate, the Ekklesia had the final decisions in all matters affecting the supreme interests of the state, as war, peace, alliances, treaties, the regulation of army and navy, finances, loans, tributes, duties, prohibition of exports or imports, the introduction of new religious rites and festivals, the awarding of honors and rewards, and the conferring of the citizenship.[24]" "In other words, the secular Ekklesia had expansive authority in determining the affairs of their cities and territories. To adequately manage these affairs, the ruling council typically met three to four times a month.[25]"

Since every Ekklesia was governed through Roman rule, their role was to activate and enforce Roman customs and laws to ensure each city looked and acted like Rome itself. Ekklesias were formed to colonize regions. They were the local ruling expression of Rome. They were apostolic in nature.

I WILL BUILD MY EKKLESIA:

Jesus could have used any word in Matthew 16:18 to define his strategy to advance His Kingdom. He could have said, I will build my bride, my temple, many synagogues, but shockingly, Jesus chooses a secular term to define His divine agency of bringing His rule and reign on the earth; the Ekklesia.

We need to clearly understand that the Kingdom of God is governmental, not religious. When Jesus came to earth, he brought his government with

---

24 A Dictionary of Classical Antiquities, Mythology, Religion, Literature and Art By Oskar Seyffer; pg. 203
25 Ekklesia Rising: The Authority of Christ in Communities of Contending Prayer by Dean Briggs pg. 111

Him (Matt 4:17). Isaiah prophesied this over 700 years before Christ's arrival (Isaiah 9:6). God's government was legally installed through our Lord's life, death, and resurrection, then becomes visible through His followers.

The Passion Translation actually translates Matthew 16:18 correctly when it says:

> *"I give you the name Peter, a stone. And this truth of who I am will be the bedrock foundation on which I will build my church—my legislative assembly."*

The Ekklesia is the governmental assembly of Heaven on Earth that functions as a praying community, legislating and acting from our positions as sons and daughters, citizens of Heaven, and changing communities for His glory on Earth. The Ekklesia is the local expression of Heaven. It co-labors with Jesus to transform every realm of society on Earth.

When we understand the true function and depth of the Ekklesia, we can see why there was such warfare to silence its true significance. The word "Ekklesia" authorizes a company of people to establish a Kingdom in all cities and regions. This is why Jesus said, "I will build MY Ekklesia…" It's His! He is the King, and we are commissioned to make the Kingdoms of this world look like those of His. He is empowering His followers to establish His government in every fiber of culture, like yeast in dough.

If we fail to gain an Ekklesia revelation, we will just go on building the "church" as what we have been led to believe it is and will miss our assignment to build Christ's Ekklesia. The Ekklesia is His passion, His will, and our assignment. It's important to note that the word Ekklesia is not isolated to the words of Jesus. The word Ekklesia is used 115 times in the New Testament. Every reference to "church" in the New Testament is the word "Ekklesia!"

THE TARGET OF CHRIST'S EKKLESIA:

It's no coincidence that Jesus released the name and function of His divine agency, the Ekklesia, at the gates of Hades. The will of our King is to access every dark, demonic gate, freeing people from the Kingdom of darkness and into the Kingdom of light. How do we begin doing this? When we understand that Jesus wants to build His Ekklesia, and its assignment is to penetrate the gates of Hades, it soon becomes clear that the way we legislate is through prayer. Prayer must become the number one functional identity of the Ekklesia. Corporate prayer is the lifeblood and backbone of the Ekklesia. We take the authority Christ has given us and access and legislate heaven on earth.

Our prayer meetings are weak because we are misinformed about our assignment. If we believe that the measure of "church" success is attendance, and the number one priority of the "church" is what goes on INSIDE its walls, then our prayer-life becomes self-centered, our focus grows inward, and our lives grow apathetic towards the Lord and His Kingdom.

Our current understanding of "church" has cut the legs off our urgency to pray. There is little "focus" nor "fight" within its current definition. We are "bored" because we are focused largely on a pastoral rather than an apostolic mandate.

It's the complete opposite with the Ekklesia. Ekklesia's cannot survive without prayer. The commission to legislate and assault the gates of Hades starts and ends with prayer since our battle is not with flesh or blood but against principalities and powers.

When we really "get" the revelation about Christ's Ekklesia, prayer is no longer an option but a necessity. The Sunday morning service is no longer "church meeting" but an "Ekklesia gathering."

The apostles knew this. When Jesus said, I will build my "Ekklesia," they understood correctly what Jesus was saying and what they were assigned to do. Begin studying the book of Acts, and you will see how the Ekklesia functioned. The baseline of the early Ekklesia was prayer, which released divine strategies, salvation, angelic visitations and kingdom power. In a little over 1.5 years, twenty percent of the city became born-again. That's revival! That's transformation!

What if the revelation of the Ekklesia is discovered by the Body Of Christ today? How would this change our lives, our churches, and our cities? What would the church actually look like? The results and implications are far-reaching!

SO WHERE DO WE GO FROM HERE?

Allow me to give you a few thoughts to consider as we move from "church" to "Ekklesia."

- **Prayer must become the number one functional identity of the Church (Ekklesia).**

Jesus calls His house a "House of Prayer" for all nations. Jesus lives to make intercession. Why? Because we are His Ekklesia. Prayer must become central for the Ekklesia to succeed.

- **We need to function as a Bride who loves and an Ekklesia who rules.**

"The people the Bride understand their rulership, not as a Bride, but because they are also the Ekklesia, and likewise, the Ekklesia understand the critical need for intimacy not as a function of their rulership, but because they are as the Bride.[26]"

It takes a bride to love Jesus as he deserves, and it takes an Ekklesia to conquer Hades.

- **We need to look at the church as a gathering of people, living stones of the Ekklesia. These are the "called out" ones, those who govern from a place of intimacy to shift the atmosphere of cities and gain air supremacy while winning people to Jesus and moving with supernatural power.**
- **We must take a fresh look at the book of Acts and see how the Ekklesia functioned. Corporate prayer leads the advancement of the Gospel and the expansion of the Kingdom.**
- **We need to ask for the Spirit of wisdom and revelation according to Ephesians 1:17 in order to better understand Christ's Ekklesia, His ruling government on earth.**

THE EKKLESIA CARRIES THE HEART OF ITS KING:

"In *The Barbarian Way*, Erwin McManus recounts a compelling insight he gained into the history of the Douglas clan while visiting Scotland. The story begins with Robert the Bruce, the Scottish noble who famously betrayed William Wallace, as immortalized by Mel Gibson in the movie *Braveheart*. Later, after Wallace's execution, Robert the Bruce rose up to lead Scotland to freedom.

---

26 Ibid. pg. 178

"Before his death in 1329, Robert requested that when he died, his heart would be removed and travel into battle with a worthy knight during the crusades. One of his closest friends, James Douglas, honored the request. The heart of Robert the Bruce was embalmed, placed in a small container, and carried around Douglas's neck. In every battle he fought, Douglas literally carried the heart of his king into the fight. In a campaign against the Moors in Granada, Spain, Douglas was surrounded by enemies. Knowing his death was imminent, he took the heart of Robert the Bruce from around his neck and flung it into the midst of the enemy forces, shouting, 'Fight for the heart of your king![27]"

Let the Ekklesia arise and fight for the heart of its KING!

---

27 Ibid. pg. 119

Epilogue

ENCOUNTER

"And He said, 'Let Me go for the day breaks.'
But he said, 'I will not let You go unless You
bless me….So Jacob called the name of the place
Peniel: 'For I have seen God face to face, and my
life is preserved.'"

Genesis 32:26,30

Every revival in history started and was sustained by one thing, encountering God, both individually and corporately. Like the Moravians, the most effective conduit of an ongoing, sustained revival is an unrelenting pursuit of His Presence in corporate settings. Whether in Herrnhut or overseas on missions, Moravians were persistent in their desire to meet, worship, pray, and seek His face corporately. Such diligence inspired a remarkable move of God lasting generations. The first church experienced such exponential growth through continued encounters with God and discipleship that empowered people in their gifts and calling from generation to generation.

Today, God is calling us back to the innocent, pure reality and power of the great commandments, loving God and loving one another. How do we carry the message of this book forward in practical ways? One word says it all…"Encounter." The call of the watchman today is to build a culture of prayer and community for transformation and revival. Such environments facilitate encounters with God and will assist people to find Jesus and journey with Him in the "garden" of their lives.

Encounters, like Jacob wrestling with God, leave us changed. They are transformational. Whether in a church, home group, a house of prayer, or on the street, communities focused on encountering God will open the pathways for spiritual transformation and a revival that will have no end. The accountability, fellowship, and inspiration that emanates from such expressions will inspire Hebrews 10:24-25, "And let us consider one another in order to stir up love and good works, not forsaking the assembling of ourselves together, as is the manner of some, but exhorting one another, and so much the more as you see the Day approaching."

May an "Encounter" focus lead us into an "Encounter Culture," that leads to the revelation of Jesus Christ as a reality for people and the end time harvest burgeoning at our doors. As communities (churches, houses of prayer, ministries, cities, etc.) develop their culture of prayer and connect across the nations, an alert and ready bride will arise ready to receive her King. As it was in the beginning, so it shall be in the end. God is the Alpha and the Omega, the beginning and the end.

To find out more and join growing families of watchmen across the nations go to www.theglobalwatch.com.

SCRIPTURES ON WATCHMEN

WATCHMEN VERSES ON TEND "ABAD:"

Exodus 3:12, So He said, "I will certainly be with you. And this shall be a sign to you that I have sent you: When you have brought the people out of Egypt, you shall *serve* God on this mountain."

Exodus 4:22-23: 'Thus says the Lord: "Israel is My son, My firstborn. So I say to you, let My son go that he may *serve* Me. But if you refuse to let him go, indeed I will kill your son, your firstborn."

Numbers 3:7-8: "And they shall attend to his needs and the needs of the whole congregation before the tabernacle of meeting, to *do* the work of the tabernacle. Also they shall attend to all the furnishings of the tabernacle of meeting, and to the needs of the children of Israel, to *do* the work of the tabernacle."

Deuteronomy 6:13: "You shall fear the Lord your God and *serve* Him, and shall take oaths in His name."

Ezekiel 36:9: "For indeed I am for you, and I will turn to you, and you shall be *tilled* and sown."

WATCHMEN VERSES ON KEEP "SAMAR:"

Genesis 17:9, "And God said to Abraham: "As for you, you shall *keep* My covenant, you and your descendants after you throughout their generations."

Exodus 12:24-27, "And you shall *observe* this thing as an ordinance for you and your sons forever. It will come to pass when you come to the land which the Lord will give you, just as He promised, that you shall *keep* this service. And it shall be, when your children say to you, 'What do you mean by this service?' that you shall say, 'It is the Passover sacrifice of the Lord, who passed over the houses of the children of Israel in Egypt when He struck the Egyptians and delivered our households.' " So the people bowed their heads and worshiped.

Leviticus 8:35, "Therefore you shall stay at the door of the tabernacle of meeting day and night for seven days, and *keep* the charge of the Lord, so that you may not die; for so I have been commanded."

Deuteronomy 4:9, "Only take *heed* to yourself, and diligently *keep* yourself, lest you forget the things your eyes have seen, and lest they depart from your heart all the days of your life. And teach them to your children and your grandchildren."

Joshua 1:7, "Only be strong and very courageous, that you may *observe* to do according to all the law which Moses My servant commanded you; do not turn from it to the right hand or to the left, that you may prosper wherever you go."

Judges 22:2, "I also will no longer drive out before them any of the nations which Joshua left when he died, so that through them I may test Israel, whether they will *keep* the ways of the Lord, to walk in them as their fathers *kept* them, or not."

1 Kings 2:3, "And keep the charge of the Lord your God: to walk in His ways, to keep His statutes, His commandments, His judgments, and His

testimonies, as it is written in the Law of Moses, that you may prosper in all that you do and wherever you turn."

1 Kings 3:14, "So if you walk in My ways, to keep My statutes and My commandments, as your father David walked, then I will lengthen your days."

2 Kings 11:5-7, "Then he commanded them, saying, "This is what you shall do: One-third of you who come on duty on the Sabbath shall be *keeping* watch over the king's house, one-third shall be at the gate of Sur, and one-third at the gate behind the escorts. You shall *keep* the watch of the house, lest it be broken down. The two contingents of you who go off duty on the Sabbath shall *keep* the watch of the house of the Lord for the king."

2 Chronicles 6:14, ""Lord God of Israel, there is no God in heaven or on earth like You, who *keep* Your covenant and mercy with Your servants who walk before You with all their hearts."

Nehemiah 1:5-6, "And I said: 'I pray, Lord God of heaven, O great and awesome God, You who *keep* Your covenant and mercy with those who love You and observe Your commandments, please let Your ear be attentive and Your eyes open, that You may hear the prayer of Your servant which I pray before You now, day and night.'"

Psalms 17:8, "Keep me as the apple of Your eye; Hide me under the shadow of Your wings."

Psalm 25:10, "All the paths of the Lord are mercy and truth, to such as keep His covenant and His testimonies."

Proverbs 3:21-23, "**Keep** sound wisdom and discretion; So they will be life to your soul and grace to your neck. Then you will walk safely in your way, and your foot will not stumble."

Isaiah 26:2-4, "Open the gates, that the righteous nation which **keeps** the truth may enter in. You will **keep** him in perfect peace, whose mind is stayed on You, because he trusts in You. Trust in the Lord forever, for in Yah, the Lord, is everlasting strength."

Ezekiel 20:18-20, "Do not walk in the statutes of your fathers, nor observe their judgments, nor defile yourselves with their idols. I am the Lord your God: Walk in My statutes, **keep** My judgments, and do them; hallow My Sabbaths, and they will be a sign between Me and you, that you may know that I am the Lord your God."

Ezekiel 36:27, "I will put My Spirit within you and cause you to walk in My statutes, and you will **keep** My judgments and do them."

Daniel 9:4, "' "O Lord, great and awesome God, who **keeps** His covenant and mercy with those who love Him, and with those who **keep** His commandments.'"

Zechariah 3:7, ""If you will walk in My ways, and if you will **keep** My command, then you shall also judge My house, and likewise have charge of My courts."

WATCHMAN SPIRITUAL POSITION:

Deuteronomy 28:13-4, "And the Lord will make you the head and not the tail; you shall be above only, and not be beneath, if you heed the commandments of the Lord your God, which I command you today, and are careful to observe them. So you shall not turn aside from any of the words which I command you this day, to the right or the left, to go after other gods to serve them."

2 Samuel 22:34-40, "He makes my feet like the feet of deer, and sets me on my high places. He teaches my hands to make war, so that my arms can bend a bow of bronze. You have also given me the shield of Your salvation; Your gentleness has made me great. You enlarged my path under me; so my feet did not slip. I have pursued my enemies and destroyed them; Neither did I turn back again till they were destroyed. And I have destroyed them and wounded them, so that they could not rise; they have fallen under my feet. For you have armed me with strength for the battle."

Psalm 25:15 "My eyes are ever toward the Lord, for He shall pluck my feet out of the net."

Psalm 26:11-12, "But as for me, I will walk in my integrity; redeem me and be merciful to me. My foot stands in an even place; in the congregations I will bless the Lord."

Psalm 27:6 "And now my head shall be lifted up above my enemies all around me; therefore I will offer sacrifices of joy in His tabernacle; I will sing, yes, I will sing praises to the Lord."

Psalm 41:12, "As for me, You uphold me in my integrity and set me before Your face forever."

Psalm 91:1 "He who dwells in the secret place of the Most High shall abide under the shadow of the Almighty."

Psalm 125:1, "Those who trust in the Lord are like Mount Zion, which cannot be moved, but abides forever."

Ezekiel 3:17-19, "Son of man, I have made you a watchman for the house of Israel; therefore hear a word from My mouth, and give them warning from Me: When I say to the wicked, 'You shall surely die,' and you give him no warning, nor speak to warn the wicked from his wicked way, to save his life, that same wicked man shall die in his iniquity; but his blood I will require at your hand. Yet, if you warn the wicked, and he does not turn from his wickedness, nor from his wicked way, he shall die in his iniquity; but you have delivered your soul."

Habakkuk 3:19, "The Lord God is my strength; He will make my feet like deer's feet, and He will make me walk on my high hills."

Luke 10:19-20, "Behold, I give you the authority to trample on serpents and scorpions, and over all the power of the enemy, and nothing shall by any means hurt you. Nevertheless do not rejoice in this, that the spirits are subject to you, but rather rejoice because your names are written in heaven."

John 13:35, "By this all will know that you are My disciples, if you have love for one another."

Acts 4:13, "Now when they saw the boldness of Peter and John, and perceived that they were uneducated and untrained men, they marveled. And they realized that they had been with Jesus."

Acts 20:30, "Also from among yourselves men will rise up, speaking perverse things, to draw away the disciples after themselves. Therefore watch, and remember that for three years I did not cease to warn everyone night and day with tears."

Romans 13:1, "Let every soul be subject to the governing authorities. For there is no authority except from God, and the authorities that exist are appointed by God."

1 Corinthians 16:13, "Watch, stand fast in the faith, be brave, be strong. Let all that you do be done with love."

1 Timothy 2:1-4, "Therefore I exhort first of all that supplications, prayers, intercessions, and giving of thanks be made for all men, for kings and all who are in authority, that we may lead a quiet and peaceable life in all godliness and reverence. For this is good and acceptable in the sight of God our Savior, who desires all men to be saved and to come to the knowledge of the truth."

1 John 4:17 "Love is perfected among us in this: that we may have boldness in the day of judgment."

Hebrews 11:6, "But without faith it is impossible to please Him, for he who comes to God must believe that He is, and that He is a rewarder of those who diligently seek Him."

WATCHMEN IN THE END TIMES:
Isaiah 62:6-7, "I have set watchmen on your walls, O Jerusalem; they shall never hold their peace day or night. You who make mention of the Lord, do not keep silent, and give Him no rest till He establishes and till He makes Jerusalem a praise in the earth."

Luke 12:37-40, "Blessed are those servants whom the master, when he comes, will find watching. Assuredly, I say to you that he will gird himself and have them sit down to eat, and will come and serve them. And if he should come in the second watch, or come in the third watch, and find them so, blessed are those servants. But know this, that if the master of the house had known what hour the thief would come, he would have watched and not allowed his house to be broken into. Therefore you also be ready, for the Son of Man is coming at an hour you do not expect."

Mark 13:6-13, "For many will come in My name, saying, "I am He,' and will deceive many. But when you hear of wars and rumors of wars, do not be troubled; for such things must happen, but the end is not yet. For nation will rise against nation, and kingdom against kingdom. And there will be earthquakes in various places, and there will be famines and troubles. These are the beginnings of sorrows. "But **watch** out for yourselves, for they will deliver you up to councils, and you will be beaten in the synagogues. You will be brought before rulers and kings for My sake, for a testimony to them. And the gospel must first be preached to all the nations. But when they arrest you and deliver you up, do not worry beforehand, or premeditate what you will speak. But whatever is given you in that hour, speak that; for it is not you who speak, but the Holy Spirit. Now brother will betray brother to death, and a father his child; and children will rise up against parents and cause them to be put to death. And you will be hated by all for My name's sake. But he who endures to the end shall be saved."

1 Thessalonians 4:15-18, "For this we say to you by the word of the Lord, that we who are alive and remain until the coming of the Lord will by no means precede those who are asleep. For the Lord Himself will descend from heaven with a shout, with the voice of an archangel, and with the

trumpet of God. And the dead in Christ will rise first. Then we who are alive and remain shall be caught up together with them in the clouds to meet the Lord in the air. And thus we shall always be with the Lord. Therefore comfort one another with these words."

Revelation 3:3, "Remember therefore how you have received and heard; hold fast and repent. Therefore if you will not watch, I will come upon you as a thief, and you will not know what hour I will come upon you."

Transformation and History Making Stories

Victory in War: Coast Watchers of World War II:

10:30 am August 7, 1942 Paul Mason packed bags and radio transmitter, from a hideaway hill observed the landing of 20,000 marines at Lunga Point on Tulagi. From his vantage point on Bougainville Island, he could see Japanese bomber formation passing overhead directed for Lunga Point. He quickly transmitted the radio message "24 torpedo bombers headed yours." It gave the Americans 45 minutes warning before the Japanese bombers struck. The warning gave time for fighter aircraft to launch and troops to cease landing and prepare. Very few of the Japanese bombers returned.

Later that day Mason gave warning to the formation of Japanese dive-bombers heading for Lunga point. The alert gave transports time to disperse and American fighters to be ready when the bombers arrived. No ships of the landing force were damaged. By end of the day, Japanese had lost 30 of the 51 planes sent.

Due to efforts of other Coastwatchers, the first 3 Japanese air strikes on Lunga Point were significantly averted making way for landing in a critical place in the South Pacific. Guadalcanal was the turning point of the battle for the South Pacific. The actions of the coastwatchers saved Guadalcanal, and Guadalcanal saved the South Pacific."

- Coastwatchers and their actions during WWII
  o Rescued 75 prisoners of war
  o 321 downed Allied airmen,
  o 280 sailors

- o 190 missionaries and civilians
- o 100's of native people
- o In one remarkable rescue of a destroyed PT boat, saved John F. Kennedy, future president of the US[28]

Over 20,000 US marines and allied forces lives were saved that day. After a few tough battles, a few months later, in the very waters they landed, many would give their lives to the Lord and be baptized. The actions of these coast-watchers changed the course of the war in the South Pacific. Such efforts of communication in a system that created community and commitment were powerful. Not only did it save lives but it prevented the spread of Buddhism into the islands and Australia. Now Christianity is alive in these islands and in particular the Melanesian islands where so many gave their lives for this effort. Such is the legacy of those nations who have "Watchmen" posted on their walls.

SUPERNATURAL PROVISION:
ADELAIDE, AUSTRALIA

Some years ago we had established two houses of prayer in Adelaide. To our surprise the Lord began to impress on us that he wanted us to purchase a motel on Kangaroo Island off the coast of South Australia. This did not make sense! To start with it involved a two hour journey by car to the ferry, a 45 minute trip across the waters of Backstairs Passage and a further half hour drive before arriving at the property. Why would the Lord want us to

---

28 http://www.battleforaustralia.org/Theyalsoserved/Coastwatchers/Coast watchers_Guadalcanal.html

take over a motel so far away that had been shut for three years and needed restoration?

More importantly, we had no money and the asking price was Aus $900,000. We put out a fleece and approached the owner, requesting that he give us six months to raise the finance. He strongly declined our request and the whole project went into death. We determined we had misunderstood the Lord.

For the next two years we would see the property advertised and hear rumors of others wanting to purchase it. Slowly we began to realize that we had let go of the vision but the Lord had not. The Chief Watchman was watching over us, and He began to reveal that He wanted us to set up a watchtower on the island because it was a key gateway; the first place of European non-convict settlement in Australia and the first place of settlement in South Australia. At Passover in 2011 the Lord spoke that we were to press in to take possession and were to prepare an offer to submit at Pentecost, which we did. It was again rejected! The Lord, however, told us to resubmit it without any changes and to our amazement it was accepted on the day of Pentecost. We then realized the importance of obeying the Lord's timing; we had first submitted it four days before Pentecost.

We still had no money, but the promise given was that the funds would come in by the Feast of Tabernacles. We waited, watched and prayed. On the last day of the Feast we were still $250,000 short. That night we attended a Christian rally in another city. During worship the vibrator on my husband's phone went off. A text came up on the screen – a promise of the final amount. The Lord was true to his word!

Today intercessors from Australia and other nations are visiting the property renamed Kingsgate Haven, and soaking in the presence of the Lord in our new prayer room at this key Australian gateway.

The Chief Watchman watches over us. Ps 121.
Jenny Hagger
Director, Australian House of Prayer For All Nations
Adelaide, Australia

EDUCATION REFORM:
EDUCATION - REGINA LIPNICK APRIL 23, 2017

Education is one of the pillars of society where everyone is impacted. People have either attended some type of educational setting or have family and friends who have attended a public institution. When we consider education, it is one of the main structures that makeup the world. Therefore, it makes sense that God wants to move among these institutions or pillars of society.

Public education is one of the keys to transforming society. God has begun to move sovereignly among children, teachers, administrators, and school staff in the public education setting.

Prototypes are starting to be created by God in public education. God is raising up administrators, teachers, and staff in strategic places throughout the county. HE is on the move and creating these prototypes to restore prayer that was taken out of public schools in 1962 (Engel v. Vitale). It is spirit-led administrators, teachers, school staff, and students who are restoring prayer and building those prototypes in the public schools.

These new prototypes involve a new structure, a new foundation, and a new way of thinking for administrators, teachers, and school staff. In this season, God is asking us to be grounded in the supernatural; to proceed in ways, thoughts, and actions that are not only unconventional, but have never been seen. He is asking us to develop new structures, new visions, and prototypes for the future. These new patterns, new ways of thinking, and new revelations are being translated straight from heaven to school personnel. God is making this shift through worship, prayer teams, and prophetic words. Judah is leading the way. Prophetic words released over schools are shifting education.

One inner city school in Florida has started the shift. In 2014, a Christian administrator volunteered to take over the lowest-performing middle school in their district. When the principal took over the school, the staff said there was no way she would be able to get the students under control. They commented that she would never be able to stop the students from cursing or fighting. In fact, they stated that the students were running the school.

When God places us in challenging situations and on roads that have been less traveled, HE always sends those who will partner with us along the way. In this case, through divine intervention, several churches from various denominations gathered together at the school to pray during the summer when the new principal took over. Prayer teams went through each classroom and hall praying, worshiping, and pushing out the darkness. As the year progressed, the principal would invite on weekends those who knew how to pray and worship. Loyal friends and family would bring guitars and worship throughout the building. Each day, the principal would decree and declare prophetic words that were being released from such prophets as Cindy Jacobs, Dutch Sheets, and Chuck Pierce. Such words as, "This is a turnaround year," "The tide is turning," and "The God of angel armies is waring on your behalf," became the catalysts for the shift and the prototype that was being established.

It was after the prayer, prophetic words, and worship had been established that a series of divine interventions started taking place. The principal was asked to attend the local church in the community to share her heart. The congregation eagerly embraced the principal's vision and began to pray for the students and new administration.

Within days after the prayer had started, school officials visited the school saying that they couldn't explain it, but that the walls were whiter. People would sit in the foyer and say, "It feels so good in this school." During the first week of school, the teachers said that they couldn't believe how fast the students loaded the buses at the end of the day without a fight. The teachers reported that the previous year before the takeover, there were four fights on the bus ramp the first day of school.

As the superintendent began to visit the school, he noted that a transformation had indeed occurred. He acknowledged that the school was not the same. He commented that the students' behavior and the instruction that was being delivered had greatly improved. Teachers also made comments that the behavior of the students had started improving the first semester. Those same teachers who said that the principal would never be able to get the students under control, reported that they couldn't believe how much the school had improved and the behaviors of the students had changed in just one semester.

Report after report was getting back to the principal about the miraculous transformation that had started taking place at the school.

The principal was visited by a superintendent from another county and his staff. The neighboring superintendent had heard about the changes that had taken place and wanted to tour the school. During the visit, his staff had commented on how they had been to the school in previous years and were astounded at the turnaround that had taken place in just one year.

A lieutenant at the local sheriff's department asked to meet with the principal and said, "Do you know your school is the talk of the town because of the changes you have made?" Do you no longer have those student behavior problems they used to have before you took over?" He went on to ask, "Is there any way that you could go visit another middle school that we are having trouble with and talk to the administration about the changes you have made here?"

In previous years, only 15 family members would show up at student orientations. The school now has hundreds of family members showing up at the events. Parents at these events have approached the principal saying, "Have you read the latest blog about your school? The blog is reporting that the school has changed and improved quickly." and "There was a time when I would not have enrolled my child at this school, but I believe I will enroll her this year."

The feeder high schools have reported to the principal that their incoming ninth-grade students from her middle school are the most well-behaved and smartest group that they have ever seen coming from that particular middle school.

Just recently, the school was visited by the Florida Department of Education and the state's accreditation team. The spokesman for the Department of Education had visited the school in previous years before the new administration took over. The team reported that the behavior of the students now was exceptional and the instructional delivery from the teachers was the strongest that they had seen in the state. It was a remarkable change from their previous visit three years prior.

Each day, the principal makes a list of the magnificent things God has done for her school. So many divine appointments and blessings have occurred, that she has cataloged them in a book and encouraged her staff to do so as well. To this day, she continues to release prophetic words, worship, and prayer over her school. This year, she was approached by teachers who asked if they could pray around the school on Friday mornings, before the students and staff entered the building. One teacher asked if she could bring her flute to school to worship and also plant a garden that represented the heart of God. Coincidently, two teachers asked if they could partner with a local church to start a youth group in the mornings before school. When the principal met with the youth leader, he asked what she wanted him to do with the students. The principal remarked, "Teach my students how to pray. Prayer will be their saving grace." How far that school has come in just two and half years! What a wonderful time we live in.

The principal commented that what she has learned, is that God's picture is always much bigger than ours. He wants us to start creating prototypes at schools so that transformation can begin in the educational system. It is through these prototypes that His kingdom can come down and the heavens open up. The end goal is to put God back in the schools and to change the state of education. To develop educational systems that are God inspired will take one prototype at a time.

Regina Lipnick
Principal Warrington Middle School
Pensacola, Florida

70123044R00095

Made in the USA
San Bernardino, CA
25 February 2018